French Riviera

LE SOLEIL TOUTE L'ANNÉE

SUR LA CÔTE D'AZUR

APA PUBLICATIONS
Part of the Langenscheidt Publishing Group

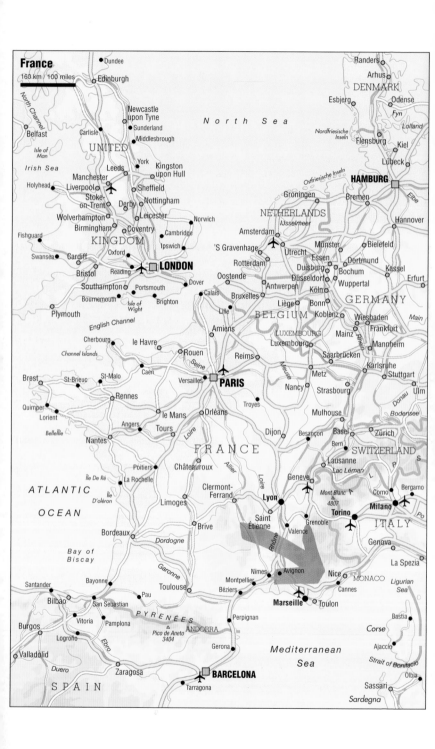

Welcome

This guidebook combines the interests and enthusiasms of two of the world's best-known information providers: Insight Guides, who have set the standard for visual travel guides since 1970, and Discovery Channel, the world's premier source of non-fiction television programming. Its aim is to bring you the best of the French Riviera in 21 tailor-made itineraries devised by Insight's correspondent in the region, Michaela Lentz.

The book begins in Nice, known as the Queen of the Riviera, from where it explores the coast east to Menton (including Monaco) and then west to Cannes. From there, it continues west to Fréjus and then St Tropez, dipping into the Massif de L'Esterel and the Massif des Maures en route. The tours can be followed individually or linked to make a grand tour; supporting them are a section on history and culture, an introduction to the region's food and wine (including restaurant recommendations), a calendar of special events and festivals, and a detailed practical information section with a list of recommended hotels.

 Michaela Lentz first came to the French Riviera in 1951, when she was fortunate enough to visit Picasso in his studio in Vallauris. The experience triggered a lasting love for the region and drew her back time and time again. Eventually she came to stay, setting up home in an old farmhouse near Vence, where she writes novels, cookery books and children's books. Although she has seen many changes over the years (as she says, 'the Côte d'Azur is loved too well by too many not to change'), her passion hasn't waned at all. The French Riviera remains one of the most alluring destinations in Europe, associated with some of the 20th century's greatest painters and writers; with fashionable Cannes, Monte Carlo and St Tropez; with high society and glamour. Michaela explores all these aspects in this guide, but also points travellers towards some of the Riviera's quieter spots, including its beautiful hinterland.

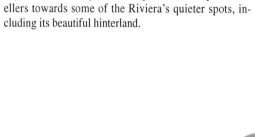

HISTORY AND CULTURE

From Roman legionaries to Matisse and Picasso, from the Counts of Toulouse to the international jet-set – an introduction to the forces and people that have left their mark on the Côte d'Azur

ITINERARIES

These 21 itineraries take you to the best of the French Riviera, beginning with Nice, Monaco and Menton and then working their way west.

contents

LEISURE ACTIVITIES

CALENDAR OF EVENTS

PRACTICAL INFORMATION

MAPS

INDEX AND CREDITS

Preceding pages: colours of the Riviera, St Tropez
Following pages: in the waters of the Côte d'Azur

NICE

History
& Culture

In the Grotto of Vallonet, near Roquebrune, archaeologists have found tools estimated to be around 900,000 years old – the oldest in France. Historical records date back to around 1000BC when a broad stretch of the Mediterranean coast was settled by the Ligurians. In 600BC Greeks from Phocaea in Asia Minor founded what is now Marseille, planting the land with olive, fig, nut and cherry trees and vines, and introducing the use of money. The city quickly prospered under these excellent traders, who went on to establish trading posts in Hyères, St Tropez, Antibes, Nice and Monaco.

Attracted by the wealth, the Celts lost no time before invading Provence, where they intermarried with the Ligurians. In 125BC Marseille appealed to Rome for help in ousting these invaders. Within three years the Romans had not only freed Marseille but conquered the whole Mediterranean region, going on to capture Aix from the Teutons in 102BC. During the first century BC Marseille supported Pompey, Caesar's rival. Caesar was victorious and removed power to Arles and Fréjus. When Caesar died, the Alps were still occupied by 44 unconquered tribes. Augustus succeeded in bringing them under Roman rule, and to commemorate the victory, in 6BC, a 40-mete (130-ft) monument was built at the foot of Mont Agel, at the meeting-point of the Via Julia and other major roads constructed during the battles. This Alpine Trophy still stands to this day at La Turbie, near Monaco.

The Via Aurelia (which followed much the same course as today's N7) was one of the most important routes in the Roman Empire. It connected Rome with Arles by way of Genoa, Cimiez (Nice), Antibes, Fréjus and Aix. Every Roman mile (1,478m/4,850ft) marker stones indicated distances. Cimiez was then the administrative capital of the *Alpes Maritimae.*

The Romans

The uncontested rule of the Romans brought the region a period of peace (the *Pax Romana*) which lasted until Provence was invaded in turn by the Vandals, Visigoths, Burgundians, Ostragoths and Franks during the 5th and 6th centuries. After this the Saracens, Moorish pirates, arrived from Spain and settled in the Massif des Maures behind Grimaud. They were expelled in 973 after terrorising the region for more than 100 years, but they continued looting the coastal areas until well into the 18th century.

Provence, declared a kingdom by Lothaire, King of the Franks, in 855, was made part of the Holy Roman Empire in the 10th century, although the Counts of Provence re-

Opposite: Nice in the 1920s
Right: Roman baths, Cimiez

tained considerable independence. Two hundred years later Provence fell first into the hands of the Counts of Toulouse and then the Counts of Barcelona, and in 1246 went to the House of Anjou when Charles of Anjou married the daughter of the Count of Barcelona. In 1308 the Grimaldi family purchased Monaco from the Genoans.

Towards the middle of the 14th century, plague ravaged Europe and the southern coast of France was not spared. After the death of the Queen of Sicily (revered as 'Pure Jeanne' by the people of Provence), Nice voted for the succession of the King of Naples. But his inability to protect the city was exploited by Count Amadeus VII from Savoy, with the result that, in 1388, Nice and its hinterland became part of the Duchy of Savoy in Italy, to which it belonged, on and off, until 1860. In contrast, the region to the west of the River Var remained part of Provence, and became French in 1486. From then on, violent confrontations between the two Côte d'Azur regions regularly erupted, until in 1860 the Duchy of Nice was finally incorporated into France.

The First Tourists

In 1864 the PLM (Paris-Lyon-Mediterranean) railway line was extended to Nice, heralding the arrival of what was to become a thriving tourist industry. The region became the winter destination of kings and queens, aristocrats and politicians, courtesans, actors and actresses, musicians and artists. In 1887 the French poet Stephen Lièvgard entitled his book about France's Mediterranean coast *La Côte d'Azur*, thus giving the landscape its name forever.

Nowadays the name Côte d'Azur conjures up images of sun and sand, yachts and beaches, intense colours and heady scents. However, foreign

Above: Nice Casino in the early years
Left: raising a glass

history/culture

visitors used to come for the autumn, winter and spring, returning home to escape from the heat of the Mediterranean summer sun. The British were largely responsible for discovering and developing the Riviera. Cannes owes its fame to Lord Brougham, who settled there in 1834. Towards the end of the 19th century Queen Victoria, whose subjects had already financed the construction of the famous Promenade des Anglais in 1820, made Nice the 'Winter Capital of the British Empire; her stay at the Hôtel Regina in Cimiez was considered the social event of the year. Meanwhile St Tropez was being transformed into a centre for painting by Paul Signac.

The Belle Epoque lifestyle of the Côte d'Azur came to an end with World War I. The Royal Highnesses now had more important matters to attend to.

Between the Wars

The 1920s on the Côte d'Azur were the *années folles*. Cole Porter was one of the first Americans to take up summer quarters, in a villa on the Cap d'Antibes. From 1923 the rich American Gerald Murphy and his wife Sara rented a villa on the Cap and gathered a clique around themselves every summer, which included Hemingway, Picasso, Léger, the Mistinguetts and, perhaps predictably, Scott and Zelda Fitzgerald.

In 1926, André Sella, owner of the Hôtel du Cap, was persuaded by his 'wild' clientele to open in the summertime. (The hotel still looks just as it did when Fitzgerald described it.) Soon convinced

of the benefits of the new fashion for sun, Sella built the Eden Roc pavilion for sun-worshippers and swimmers next door to his hotel. From then on bronzed skin became fashionable and the summer tourist industry was born on the French Riviera – a trend that gained ground in 1936 when the French government introduced paid holidays.

At around this time a newly married millionaire couple appeared in Cannes on their honeymoon: Frank and Florence Gould. On an outing the two discovered a pine grove and beach next to the little village of Juan-les-Pins. Florence then bought all the land and built on it first a casino and then the Hôtel Le Provençal, soon to be a serious rival to the Hôtel du Cap.

She also built a villa which she extravagantly transformed into a neo-Gothic castle. There the Goulds received not only *le beau monde*, but also famed French authors of the time. Benoit, Gide, Morand, Montherlant, Giraudoux, Louise de Vilmorin, as well as Scott and Zelda Fitzgerald were, from 1924 on, among the guests who attended many wild and boisterous parties. This was the decade of Gatsby abroad, the era immortalised in such books as Fitzgerald's *Tender is the Night*.

For more than half a century the Goulds ruled over Juan-les-Pins and Cannes, where they acquired Villa Le Patio. In rooms containing paintings by artists such as Van Gogh and Matisse, they entertained Film Festival stars and other promi-

Above: a poster advertising La Route Bleue, the stylish way to travel

nent people. In 1961 General de Gaulle honoured Mrs Gould for meritorious patronage. She died in 1983 aged88.

Back to the year 1925, Colette, the author of *Claudine in Paris* and *Gigi*, fell in love with St Tropez. Visitors to her house (La Treille Muscate, situated in the middle of a vineyard) included Lucien Guitry, Dunoyer de Segonzac, Jean-Pierre Aumont, Jeff Kessel, Saint Exupéry, Cocteau, Simone Simon and Marc Allégret.

Romance Blooms

'Miss France, 1930' was a tall, slim young woman from Cannes called Yvette. Not far from the fashion salon in which Yvette worked, the Aga Khan, who frequently visited Cannes, amused himself playing skittles. They eventually met and Yvette became ' one of the richest women in the world. The couple lived in Le Cannet in the Villa Yakimour – *Y* for Yvette, *mour* as in *amour*. After the death of her husband in 1957, Yvette largely withdrew from society, but for years she could still often be seen out walking in Cannes.

In December 1936, some 200 international journalists awaited the arrival of Wallis Simpson, the American woman who, as the world was shortly to find out, was worth more to a king than his throne. On 12 December 1936 King Edward VIII abdicated, and the twice-divorced Wallis listened to this declaration of love in her Villa Viei. Six months later the couple were married, making their home the Château de la Croë on the Cap d'Antibes.

War and After

World War II kept visitors away from the Riviera. Nice's historical links with Italy inspired Mussolini to bring the south-eastern tip of France 'home' to Italy, and the Italians occupied Menton in 1940. After the split between Germany and Italy in 1943, the Germans took over the occupation. The Resistance movement was active in the region, repatriating escaped prisoners and shot-

down air crews. Allied troops liberated Provence in August 1944, landing on the beaches between Toulon and the Esterel.

In 1946 Picasso came to live in Antibes, where he painted as if possessed. His large-scale work named *Joie de Vivre* said it all – the war was finally over, the pleasures of life were well and truly back. In the early 1950s he transformed the Roman chapel in Vallauris into a monument to peace with his work *La Guerre et la Paix* (War and Peace). Meanwhile, Matisse was working on the chapel in Vence and Chagall painted his *Messages Bibliques*.

St Tropez welcomed its most famous resident: Brigitte Bardot. Soon her fame was such that she could no longer go for walks along the harbour or go shopping in the narrow alleyways of the town without being recognised, and often whistled at or harassed, by tourists. They even showed up in boats, drifting past her villa La Madrague.

In Monaco, Prince Rainier III orientated the Principality's economy towards the American example – commercialising caviar and hot-dogs to the same degree. He also gained the love of a woman who gave up a successful career as an actress to marry him in 1956. As Grace Kelly she was a Hollywood star; however, she played her biggest and brightest role in Monaco.

Modern Development

Since then, much has changed on the Côte d'Azur. The Promenade des Anglais is now a superhighway. Those who wish to visit St Tropez (and cannot afford to rent a helicopter) will get stuck for hours in the traffic jams. The railway tracks no longer belong to the private trains of the upper crust, but rather to the fastest train in the western world: the TGV speeds along at 270km (170 miles) per hour. Once the Côte d'Azur was the playground of the privilaged few; now approximately 10 million tourists visit here annually. Tourism has made the region famous, brought affluence, and defined its modern face. It's the basis of the economy. Business and congress tourism are still increasing, with hotel beds now filled year-round.

In an attempt to avoid the monoculture of tourism the Côte has encouraged non-polluting high-tech industry to establish bases there. Projects which reflect this decision include the research centre of the information-processing giant IBM in La Gaude and the ambitious Sophia Antipolis science park near Valbonne, one of Europe's leading technology parks. Vast sums of money are also being poured into luxury real-estate. The Villa Trianon on Cap Ferrat cost the late Christina Onassis 800,000 francs in rent per month. The Fabris, Rizzolis and Mondadoris have bought into the Cap as well. Villas sell for 20 to 30 million US dollars.

These examples illustrate the scale of the development that has taken place in the region. Even so, there is considerably more to the French Riviera than the bravura of the coastal strip. Coast and hinterland are two extremes which nonetheless have a unity in their contrasts. But even such a blessed area as the Côte d'Azur has its problems. Inland, fire is the feared enemy of the forests, most of them caused by the heat of summer, dry-

Above left: the Goulds, fashionable hosts in the 1930s.
Left: at Gran Hôtel du Cap-Eden Roc. **Right**: Bardot

ness, coniferous woods and underbrush, the unpredictable *Mistral* wind, care-lessness and lack of investment in preventative measures. Fire fighting is carried out by Canadair water-bombers stationed in Marignane. Groups of green-helmeted young men, equipped with walkie-talkies, patrol the endangered areas on motorcycles, but fire remains one of the greatest dangers throughout the entire Mediterranean basin, and visitors are asked to bear this in mind.

The Balls Keep Rolling

The call *Faites vos jeux! Rien ne va plus* was heard for the first time in Monaco in 1863. Since then many have succumbed to a fascination with the little tumbling ball. Winston Churchill made his first appearance in the Casino in 1939. He returned in 1949 and, playing at the same table as 10 years previously, won

2 million francs. The balls are still rolling thanks in particular to wealthy Italian punters visiting from Turin and Milan. Meanwhile, banks of one-armed bandits have also been installed, and tourists can try their luck on these in the afternoons. Slot machines at such venues as the Casino Ruhl and Monte Carlo Casino open as early as 10am.

A little ball also plays a considerable role in the most popular game of Southern France. In *boules* or *pétanque* one of the players throws the smallest ball – the wooden *bouchon* for a distance of up to 20 metres (60ft). With the next throw he tries to get his metal ball as close as possible to the *bouchon*. A player of the other team then strives to get his ball still closer. The opponents take turns in their endeavours. The hollow, deep thwack of one ball hitting another is one of the most evocative sounds of the Côte d'Azur.

From Bréa to César

The Nice School flourished between 1450 and 1570, a style of painting which can be compared in significance with that of Siena. The works of these painters, primarily employed by the Order of Penitent Monks, can be found in many of the pilgrimage churches and chapels in and around Nice, for example in Peille, Biot, Tourettes-sur-Loup, Bar-sur-Loup, Bouyon and Le Broc. The best known painter of altar images and frescoes from this period was Louis Bréa. He was born in Nice and was called the 'Provençal Fra Angelico', probably because of the naive uprightness, sincerity, humanity and simplicity with which he imbued his subjects. His brother Antoine, nehew François, Jean Miralheti, Jacques Durandi, Jean Canavesio, Jean Baleison and André de la Cella also belonged to *les primitifs niçcois*.

In the 1950s and 1960s a second School of Nice came into being. Among its members are Arman, Ben, Chubac, Farhi, Gilly, Klein, Malaval, Morabito, Slobodan, Sosno and César.

HISTORY HIGHLIGHTS

30,000BC Evidence of early *homo sapiens* in cave paintings in Grotte Cosquer, near Cassis.

1000BC Ligurians occupy the Mediterranean coast.

600BC Marseille founded by the Greeks.

121BC Founding of Roman town of Aquae-Sextiae, now Aix-en-Provence.

118BC Founding of first Gallo-Roman province, Provincia (Provence).

102BC Invading German tribes defeated.

14BC Ligurians and other tribes defeated by Emperor Augustus.

AD476 Collapse of the Roman Empire.

536 Franks take over Provence.

855 French king, Charles the Bald, rules the Kingdom of Provence.

1032 Provence becomes part of Holy Roman Empire.

1186 Aix becomes capital of Provence.

1248 The Seventh Crusade is launched from Aigues-Mortes by Louis IX.

1308 Grimaldi family purchase Monaco from Genoa.

1309 The Papacy flees Rome to take up residence in Avignon.

1334–52 Construction of the Palais des Papes in Avignon.

1377 After seven French popes, an Italian is elected and returns to Rome. The French choose a rival pope in Avignon and papal schism results.

1388 Nice becomes part of Duchy of Savoy, ruled from Italy.

1434–80 Reign of Good King René.

1481 Charles du Maine hands over Provence to the king of France.

1486 Union of Provence with France.

1539 French becomes official language in Provence.

1545–98 Wars of Religion, ended by Edict of Nantes. Protestants massacred in Provence.

1718 Nice becomes part of Sardinia.

1720 The Plague ravages Provence.

1789 French Revolution. Storming of the Bastille.

1793 Napoleon breaks the English siege of Toulon, and quickly rises to power.

1814 Napoleon lands at Golfe Juan.

1820 Construction of the Promenade des Anglais in Nice.

1834 Lord Brougham settles in Cannes.

1860 Union of Nice with France

1861 Roquebrune and Menton ceded to France by Monaco.

1863 First casino opens in Monte Carlo.

1864 Paris-Lyon-Mediterranean railway line extended to Nice.

1879 Monte Carlo opera is opened.

1887 Poet Stephen Liègard christens the Côte d'Azur in a book of that title.

1892 Impressionist artist Paul Signac discovers St Tropez.

1906 Renoir arrives to live in Cagnes.

1909 First winter sports in Nice region.

1911 Carlton Hotel built in Cannes.

1924 Scott and Zelda Fitzgerald visit the Riviera.

1925 Arrival of Coco Chanel, who introduces the fashion for sunbathing. Colette moves to St Tropez.

1929 First Monaco Grand Prix.

1936 Introduction of paid holidays for workers; mass tourism begins.

1940 Italians occupy Alpes Maritimes.

1944 Allied landings between Toulon and Esterel.

1946 First Cannes Film Festival. Picasso painting in Antibes.

1956 Brigitte Bardot stars in *And God Created Woman* in St Tropez.

1956 Grace Kelly marries Prince Rainier of Monaco.

1970 Completion of Autoroute du Soleil.

1973 Picasso dies in Mougin.

1982 Car accicdent kills Princess Grace of Monaco.

1990 Musée d'Art Contemporain opens in Nice.

2000 TGV extension proposed along the coast to Nice; local residents protest.

history/culture

Nice

1.6 km / 1 mile

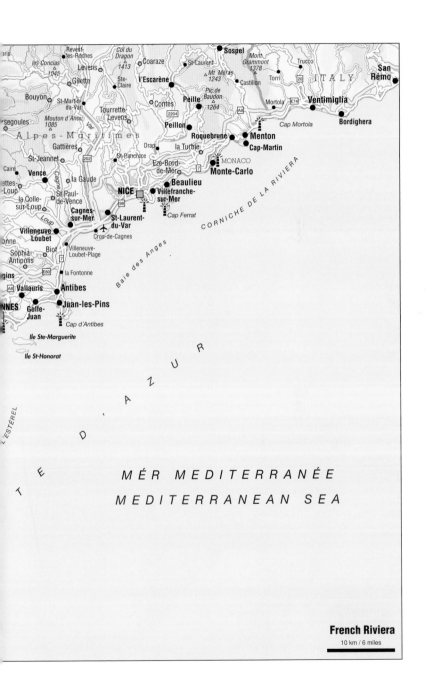

les Concias
Revest-
les-Roches
Col du
Dragon
1413
Coaraze
St-Laurent
Sospel
Mont
Grammont
1378
Trucco
San
Rémo
Levens
1045
Gilette
Ste-
Claire
l'Escarène
Mt. Méras
1243
Castillon
Torri
20
ITALY
Bouyon
St-Martin-
du-Var
Tourrette-
Levens
Contes
Peille
Pic de
Baudon
1264
A8
Mortola
E74
Ventimiglia
segoules
Mouton d'Anou
1085
Var
Peillon
2204
Cap Mortola
Bordighera
Alpes-Maritimes
Gattières
Drap
Roquebrune
Menton
Caire
St-Jeannet
202
St-Pancrace
la Turbie
Cap-Martin
Vence
la Gaude
Eze-Bord-
de-Mer
7
MONACO
Monte-Carlo
ettes-
Loup
la Colle-
sur-Loup
St-Paul-
de-Vence
NICE
Beaulieu
Villefranche-
sur-Mer
CORNICHE DE LA RIVIERA
Cagnes-
sur-Mer
98
Villeneuve
Loubet
St-Laurent-
du-Var
Cros-de-Cagnes
Cap Ferrat
onne
Biot
Villeneuve-
Loubet-Plage
Baie des Anges
Sophia-
Antipolis
7
gins
E80
la Fontonne
A8
Vallauris
Antibes
NNES
Golfe-
Juan
Juan-les-Pins
Cap d'Antibes
Ile Ste-Marguerite
Ile St-Honorat

L'ESTEREL

C Ô T E   D ' A Z U R

MÉR MEDITERRANÉE

MEDITERRANEAN SEA

French Riviera
10 km / 6 miles

Orientation

The region covered by this guide is bordered by Menton in the east and St Tropez in the west (for an overview, see the pull-out map accompanying this guide). Nice has been chosen as the point of departure for this book because it is the capital city of the French Riviera, as well as the location of the international airport (the second-busiest in France). Not by chance has this city become a major tourist centre.

East of Nice

If you appreciate fashionable society, Monte Carlo, the gambling capital of Europe, provides a unique milieu. Understated elegance awaits visitors to Beaulieu, Cap Ferrat, Cap Martin and Menton on the Basse Corniche, the coastal road from Nice to the Italian border (*see page 27*) You can also reach Menton from Nice via the Moyenne Corniche (*see pages 34*), which has magnificent views over the sea and the coastal villages and is, moreover, the quickest route to Eze, one of the region's best preserved medieval mountain villages. Visitors interested in history might prefer the Grande Corniche (*see pages 37*), which partly follows the course of the ancient Via Julia Augusta, and gives you the chance to visit Roquebrune (a fortified town from the Carolingian period) and the famous Roman victory monument, the Alpine Trophy.

West of Nice

The route from Nice to Vence leads through hinterlands which have largely been spared the hubbub of tourism. As well as giving a glimpse of genuine Provençal countryside, it takes you to Haut-de-Cagnes, where you can see Renoir's beautiful garden. Around Vence you can explore charming landscapes and unspoiled mountain villages. The modern art in the stylish Fondation Maeght should, ideally, be followed by a meal at the legendary Colombe d'Or. Both are in St Paul-de-Vence and are unforgettable.

The drive from Nice to Cannes is rich with possibilities: the Escoffier Museum in Villeneuve-Loubet; the yachting harbour and Picasso museum in Antibes; the secluded bays of Cap d'Antibes; the nightlife of Golfe Juan and Juan-les-Pins; ceramics wherever you cast your eye in Picasso's Vallauris; and the glass-blowing workshop in Biot. Next comes Cannes, hub of high society. From here you can make an excursion out to the Lérins Islands, or follow the tracks of Napoleon through Mougins (with its renowned restaurants) to the centre of the perfume industry at Grasse.

After Cannes, the Corniche de L'Esterel begins: red cliffs of volcanic stone; indented capes and little sandy bays. Along this stretch is St Raphaël, once described as a 'stately, old-fashioned Riviera town', and, next to it, Fréjus, on the Via Aurelia, with its Roman relics and medieval cathedral quarter.

Left: Villefranche, the quintessential Riviera town
Right: follow the signs

1. THE RIVIERA'S GRANDE DAME *(see map below)*

The Promenade des Anglais; a drink at the Hôtel Negresco; the town centre and its luxury boutiques; the old town; the harbour; Roman Cimiez and the Musée Chagall.

Allow a full day for this tour. The starting point is the western end of the Promenade des Anglais

Nikaia, Nice, Nissa-la-Bella or simply l'Olive, the *Grande Dame* of the Riviera, as it was known in its Golden Age, the era of crinolines, empresses (Eugénie) and queens (Victoria), has filled out somewhat since the 19th century. With a population of around 400,000, the city has spread back from the sea over the surrounding hills, and west as far as the airport. The **Promenade des Anglais**, so-named because the English were responsible for its construction, follows the broad sweep of the Baie des Anges. Despite the heavy traffic that has replaced the pedestrians who once sauntered along in the shade of the palms, the Promenade still manages to keep something of its original splendour.

'If you would like to see the most beautiful land in the world, here it is.' So wrote painter Pierre Auguste Renoir to Berthe Morisot, while simultaneously qualifying his praise: 'In winter, of course, it occurs to me that it's more like some kind of hot-house into which people with fragile health take refuge.' Here he is referring to the mistaken notion then prevalent that the mild climate of the

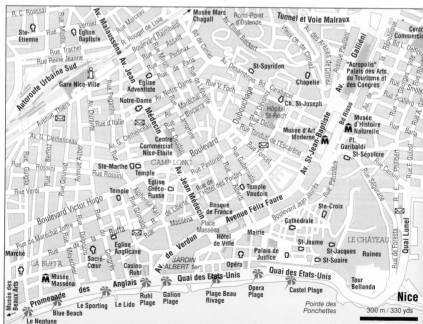

Côte would be therapeutic to people with lung complaints, an error which, well into the 19th century, misled many people into spending their winters here, or even settling permanently. More caustically, De Maupassant called the town: '...a hospital of the *monde*, death's waiting room, the blooming graveyard of Europe's high nobility.'

It wasn't until the 20th century that Nice began to free itself from dependence on tourism. The airport – now the second busiest in France – was built in 1957, the university founded in 1965, and various colleges, convention centres, arts centres and museums have followed.

Museums and the Belle Epoque

First stop on the Promenade is the **Musée International d'Art Naïf Anatole Jakovsky** (Château Sainte-Hélène, Avenue de Fabron, tel: 04 93 71 78 33; 10am–6pm; closed Tues and some bank holidays). This is the richest museum of its kind in the world, with an inventory of some 1,000 paintings sourced from 27 countries. The 300 works on permanent display, donated by the collector and art critic Jakovsky, are done full justice in the bright rooms of the castle. Also at this end of the Promenade des Anglais is **Phoenix Park**, combining glorious gardens with the sleek **Asian Arts Museum** (tel: 04 92 29 37 00; 10am–5pm, or 6pm from 2 May–15 Oct; closed Tues and some bank holidays) at its heart.

The **Musée des Beaux Arts** at 33 Avenue des Baumettes (tel: 04 92 15 28 28; 10am–noon and 2–6pm; closed Mon and some bank holidays) is well worth a visit. Here the main theme is painting of the 19th century. Modern art is scarcely represented, with the exception of the Dufy Collection, which is exhibited on a rotating basis.

Back on the Promenade, continue eastwards to the beautiful **Hôtel Negresco**, Nice's most famous landmark. Sitting on the terrace with a drink or ice cream is an enjoyable way to admire the hotel's Belle Epoque architecture. Just behind the Negresco is the **Musée d'Art et d'Histoire Palais Masséna** (65 Rue de France/35 Promenade des Anglais, tel: 04 93 88 11 34; closed for restoration until 2005), showing local history and the works of Bréa and Durandi, two of the earlier masters of Nice.

A little further on is the **Jardin Albert I** with refreshing fountains; concerts are held here in summer. This is the boarding-point for a mini-train that leaves every 30 minutes on a tour of the old town, the flower market and the castle gardens; a double-decker tourist bus, departing every one to two hours and taking in the port, Mt Boron and Cimiez, also leaves from here.

The Turin-style **Place Masséna** represents the centre of the city these days, its fountains bordered by elegant red façades, a reminder that Nice is

Above left: Hôtel Negresco
Above right: pausing on the Promenade des Anglais

historically more Italian than French. This is the hub for luxury boutiques: designer names are on display in every window with prices to match. **Avenue Jean Médecin** to the north of the square is the main shopping street. Here you will find Galeries Lafayette, France's biggest department store chain, and Nice Etoile, a big shopping centre. The **Rue Masséna/Rue de France** is a pedestrian zone lined with busy terrace cafés and restaurants as well as shops.

Old Town and Harbour

Leaving modern Nice, head for the old town and the harbour, which are located on the other side of the Paillon River. The area around the river was the heart of the town's activity during the last century, but the river can no longer be seen. It has been bridged over by squares, avenues, and the **Acrop-**

olis arts, convention and exhibition centre which is anchored in the river-bed by five immense arches. Both the exterior and interior of the Acropolis are decorated with the works of contemporary artists (Volti, Vasarely, Arman, César and others), which harmonise well with the architectural style. A new theatre and museum of modern art, the **Musée d'Art Moderne et Contemporain** (Promenade des Arts, tel 04 93 62 61 62; 10am–6pm; closed Mon and some bank holidays) complete this important complex.

La Vieille Ville, called the *babazouk* in Niçois dialect, is the picturesque heart and soul of Nice. This is the authentic Nissa-la-Bella, a true delight for the senses. Here, the alleys are narrow and the houses tall; the facades are colourfully ornamented

Above: Cours Saleya flower market
Left: Nice's old town

with flowers and laundry hung out to dry; the typical hubbub of all Mediterranean communities is in evidence here throughout the day.

From the Acropolis (from which you can walk all the way down to the sea through a series of gardens known as the **Promenade des Arts**), head for **Place Garibaldi**, which is surrounded by houses with loggias. The plaza is named in memory of the Italian nationalist Giuseppe Garibaldi (1807–82), who was born here. Nearby is the **Eglise St Martin-St Augustin**, the oldest parish church in Nice in which Luther celebrated mass and Garibaldi was baptised. Across the street is a monument erected to Catherine Ségurane, who hitched her skirts up high and fought back the Turks with a knife in 1543.

The famous Nice fish market, where fishermen and fishwives loudly advertise the day's catch, takes place every morning (except Monday) on the **Place St François**. As you stroll around the old town, look up and admire the façades painted with frescoes and *trompe l'oeil*, the most famous of which can be seen as you drive down the **Quai des Etats-Unis** from east to west – depicting a man stood on a ladder painting a palm tree on the wall. Not so many years ago the old town was in a state of neglect; the municipality has recently stepped in with a major restoration project. One beneficiary is the **Place Rossetti**, around the **Cathédrale Ste Réparate**, where the façades have been repainted in hues of red, pink, ochre and yellow. Nearby, in Rue Droite, is the **Palais Lascaris** (tel: 04 93 62 72 40; 10am–6pm; closed Tues and 15 days in Nov), a magnificent baroque palace once belonging to the Lascaris-Ventimiglia family and now a local museum.

Flowers and Bric-a-Brac

The **Cours Saleya** lies between the old city and the sea. In the 19th century it served as the principal meeting-place for high society; today it is a hive of activity from morning to night. Its famous flower market is open every day except Monday, when it gives way to an antiques and bric-a-brac market. Monday is the best day to reserve a table for lunch at **Safari**, which specialies in local dishes; you can observe the crowds from a ringside seat.

The Cours Saleya is separated from the sea by the Ponchettes, once the wharf arsenal of the Savoyard-Sardinian navy, and from the rest of the old town by the **Préfecture**, formerly the palace of the Sardinian kings and, until the mid 1990s, the official home of the discredited mayor of Nice, the late Jacques Médécin. From the Cours Saleya, head off up the 90-metre (300-ft) hill between the old town and the harbour, the old citadel still known as the **Château** (though no castle has stood there for nearly 300 years), which offers a panoramic view of the Baie des Anges and the city.

The city authorities have provided several ways up: for those who can climb them, there are steps; there is also a lift; or you can stroll up the winding path from the Rue Ségurane to the highest point. In the beautifully located cemetery, which you pass on the way back down, is the grave of the daughter of Consul Emil Jellinek. The name doesn't mean anything to you? Well, Jellinek won the Nice-Magnan car rally in 1899 in a Daimler, which he christened after his daughter Mercedes.

Right: street entertainment

Crossing the Rue Ségurane, wander down towards the harbour. You will find yachts and fishing-boats moored here, as well as excursion ships and boats for rent. Car ferries to Corsica leave almost daily from the outer harbour. On the Quai des Deux Emmanuel is the gourmet restaurant **L'Esquinade**.

Roman Centre

Cimiez (in Roman times *Cemenelum*) can be best reached via the Boulevard de Cimiez, the route also taken by the coaches of the Belle Epoque when the

guests of the Winter Palace and the hotels Ermitage, Alhambra and Regina returned from the sea back up to their hill.

In the 1st century BC, after the conquest of the Alpes Maritimes, which represented an important communication route to Gaul and Spain, the Romans constructed the Via Julia Augusta along the coast, and on the hills of Cimiez they erected their own town of *Cemenelum*. It was intended to rival the existing Greek town of Nikaia (whose name eventually became Nice). As well as the splendid architecture of the Belle Epoque you can see the recent excavations of Roman ruins, which include an amphitheatre (where one of the world's best jazz festivals takes place every July) and Roman baths from the 3rd century.

Off the **Place du Monastère** is the cemetery where Raoul Dufy (1877–1953), Henri Matisse (1869–1954) and the writer Martin du Gard are buried. Cimiez is also home to several museums, including the **Musée d'Archéologie** (160 Avenue des Arènes, tel: 04 93 81 59 57; 10am–6pm Apr–Sep; closed Tues and some bank holidays), where further evidence of the Roman occupation is displayed.

Fine Arts Too

One of several important fine arts museums is the **Musée Nationale Marc Chagall** (on the corner of Boulevard de Cimiez and Avenue Dr Ménard, tel: 04 93 53 87 20; 10am–5pm, or 6pm July–Sep; closed Tues and some bank holidays), which was designed to house Chagall's masterpiece *Messages Bibliques*, and the biggest single collection of the artist's work.

The **Musée Matisse** in the Villa des Arènes (164 Avenue des Arènes, tel: 04 93 81 08 08; 10am–5pm, or 6pm Apr–Sep; closed Tues and some bank holidays) has been renovated with a modern extension, and shows the development of this versatile artist with paintings, drawings, prints and bronze figures, as well as displaying many of his personal possessions. Matisse lived in Nice for 20 years, at one time on the Cours Saleya, and latterly in the Hôtel Regina, which had been built for Queen Victoria in 1897.

Above: the baroque Palais Lascaris

There are three roads between Nice and Menton: the Basse Corniche follows the beautiful stretch of coast, but can be busy especially in summer, the Moyenne Corniche is the fastest, and the Grande Corniche is for nature-lovers and picnickers.

2. THE BASSE CORNICHE *(see map, p28)*

Villefranche: fish at La Mère Germaine; the medieval Rue Obscure; St Jean-Cap-Ferrat: the Billionaires' Peninsula; a walk around the cape; Beaulieu.

The distance between Nice and Menton via the Basse Corniche (N98) is 31km (20 miles). Allow half a day for this tour, including stops

'At this place between heaven and earth the world stands still.' So Maurice Maeterlinck, winner of the 1911 Nobel Prize for Literature, described the white and ochre palace with which he fell immediately in love, in his work *Les Sept Fées d'Orlamondé*. Today the **Palais Maeterlinck** is one of Nice's most exclusive hotels. Although the rooms are beyond the budget of most of us, the restaurant is open to the public and offers splendid views from Cap Ferrat to Cap d'Antibes. It is located just as you leave Nice of the Basse Corniche going towards Villefranche.

Villefranche (Free City) is on one of the most beautiful inlets of the Mediterranean. Where the yachts and sporting boats drop anchor to-day there was once a naval port in which galleys were constructed and in whose deep waters the Queen of France unexpectedly went swimming in 1538 when the gangplank to her ship collapsed. The tall, colourful façades of the old town line the attractive fishing harbour, which is one of the most pleasant settings in the region for a leisurely lunch. Several restaurants have terraces overlooking the water, but my favourite, and also that of Jean Cocteau, is **La Mère Germaine**, which serves excellent fish dishes.

The picturesque tangle of alleys and steps, and the arched **Rue Obscure** dating from the 13th century have barely changed since the Middle Ages. On the quayside is the **Chapelle St Pierre** which was decorated

Above: Villefranche and the Citadel
Right: sculpture in the Citadel courtyard

by Jean Cocteau, who grew up in Villefranche, in 1957. The **Hôtel Welcome**, where the artist sometimes resided, is thoroughly recommended.

The **Citadel**, which was built at the end of the 16th century for the protection of the bay, houses the **Musée Goetz-Boumeester** (tel: 04 93 76 33 44; 9am–noon and 2–5.30pm; closed Tues and Sun morning and Nov), displaying abstract paintings as well as works of Picasso, Miró and Hartung. In the same complex is the **Fondation Musée Volti** (opening times as Musée Goetz-Boumeester), dedicated to local artists. It features sculptures of female figures displayed in the courtyard.

The Billionaires' Peninsula

From the **Pont St Jean** take a drive round **Cap Ferrat** – sometimes known as the 'Billionaires' Peninsula'. The 10-km (6-mile) road takes you past high hedges and sturdy gates, behind which you catch glimpses of beautifully preserved villas set in well-tended parkland. Former residents include King Leopold II of Belgium, who chose the site because of its reputation for having the most pleasant climate in France. On his 14-hectare (35-acre) estate, Les Cèdres, he built a palace for himself and three villas for his mistresses. In 1926 Somerset Maugham bought the Villa Mauresque, which was built by the king's confessor Monsignor Charmeton.

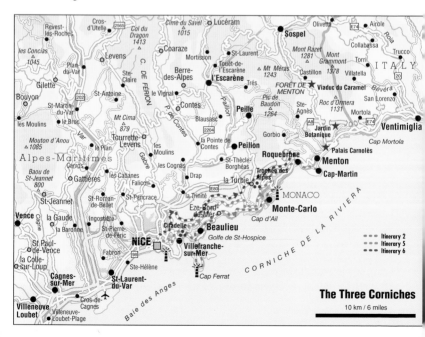

The Three Corniches

10 km / 6 miles

Itinerary 2
Itinerary 5
Itinerary 6

2. the basse corniche

east of nice

Also on the Cap is the former residence of the Baroness Ephrussi de Rothschild, the **Villa Ephrussi-Rothschild** (tel: 04 93 01 45 90; Feb–June and Sep–Oct, 10am–6pm; July and Aug 10am–7pm; Nov–Mar, 10am–6pm Mon–Fri and 10am–6pm weekends and school holidays), which she had built to house her private art collection. The beautiful Italian-style palace now belongs to the state and is open as a museum, displaying mainly 18th-century Italian furniture, porcelain, carpets and paintings.

Edith Piaf also had a house on the Cap, the Villa Sospiro, as did David Niven and, more recently, the Rolling Stones and Tina Turner. It is thanks to these villas, often unoccupied and well-protected by dogs and heavily-armed bodyguards, that the beauty and quiet of the peninsula has been preserved. Among the most impressive residences are the Maryland, the Vigie, Mes Roches and Serena, all located on **Passable Beach**, a sandy beach that slopes gently down to the sea, and from which you can take a shady footpath leading round to the village of **St Jean-Cap-Ferrat**. This thoroughfare is the former customs road, and along the way you will find small, uncrowded inlets, ideal for swimming. A splendid view rewards those with the courage to climb the 164 steps to the lighthouse, one of the most modern in France. At the tip of the peninsula is a tower which served as a jail in the 18th century.

St Jean itself is little more than a tiny harbour lined with a few cafés and old houses, and despite modernisation it has managed to retain its picturesque charm. The Voile d'Or is a delightful restaurant overlooking the harbour.

Beaulieu is among the warmest places on the French Riviera. If you feel like a stroll, the **Maurice Rouvier Promenade** leads around the Baie des Fourmis past luxurious villas to St Jean-Cap Ferrat. Alternatively, for the more energetic, the footpath to the **Plateau St Michel** is a steep climb up the escarpment, affording beautiful views on the way. Allow a good hour and a half there and back. The **Villa Kerylos** (Impasse Eiffel, tel: 04 93 01 01 44; Sep, Oct and Feb–June, 10am–6pm; July and Aug 10am–7pm; Nov–Jan, Mon–Fri 2–6pm and 10am–6pm weekends and school holidays), a reconstruction of an ancient Greek villa, is worth a visit.

Afterwards head for **Eze Bord-de-Mer**, from where you can climb up to **Eze** village on foot, as Nietzsche did while conceiving the third part of *Thus Spake Zarathustra*. This is one of the French Riviera's most dramatic hilltop villages (*see page 35*). Then, travelling by way of the **Cap d'Ail**, with secluded villas among fir trees and cypresses on the lower cliffs of the **Tête de Chien** ('Dog's Head', a reference to its shape), you will arrive at **Monaco**.

Left: Villa Ephrussi-Rothschild
Above: Villa Kerylos

3. MONACO *(see map, p32)*

The Old City: the Cathedral, the Musée Océanographique, the Place de Palais; the Jardin Exotique; the Casino. Tips for Monte Carlo by day and by night.

Starting point is the Cathedral in Monaco. Allow a full day

Descendants of the Grimaldi family live in Cagnes, Beuil, Naples and Genoa. It was Francesco Grimaldi, driven out of Genoa, who took control of Monaco in 1297 in a coup in which he and his accomplices disguised themselves as monks. Although he was unable to hold Monaco, to this day the armed monk in the Grimaldi coat of arms stands as a reminder of the coup. In 1308 the Grimaldi family bought Monaco from the Genoese. The history of the Principality is fraught with family strife and a series of occupations by various powers, including the Spanish, the French and the Sardinians.

In 1861 Roquebrune and Menton, until then part of the state, were incorporated into France, leaving Monaco much smaller and poorer. In an attempt to attract aristocratic tourism, Prince Charles III decided to turn Monaco into a health and leisure resort and to allow gambling, which was forbidden in neighbouring countries. He eliminated direct taxation and created Monte Carlo, where, in 1863, he built a small casino. Although this did not solve his financial problems immediately, the situation changed when François Blanc bought the casino and, with several associates, founded the **Société des Bains de Mer** (SBM). Before long a new city evolved around the casino, with palatial hotels, villas and magnificent grounds. Towards the end of the 19th century wealthy guests started to arrive, although only in winter at first. Today there are several million visitors a year.

The Influence of Grace

In the 1950s Aristotle Onassis was the controlling shareholder of the exclusive SBM. Meanwhile, under the influence of Princess Grace, Prince Rainier III adopted an American-style of marketing to open up the Principality to tourists. Over the years the SBM has grown into a gigantic enterprise, and its

restaurants have amassed six Michelin stars. Two of these stars were won by chef Alain Ducasse of the Louis XV restaurant in the **Hôtel de Paris**; his former apprentice Caironi has been awarded one for the Grill, also in the Hôtel de Paris; another went to Garnier at La Coupole in **Hôtel Mirabeau**.

The Principality is now a tax-paradise for a privileged few: indeed, the Prince grants fewer than 300 applications for citizenship each year. Boris Becker, Alain Prost and Bjorn Borg are among the lucky ones. The British writer Anthony Burgess punched the keys of his old Remington typewriter here until his death in 1994.

It is one of the Principality's attractions that its 30,000 inhabitants (of whom scarcely more than 5,000 are genuine *Monégasques*) live in total security. The video observation system in Monaco is as discreet as it is effective, and it is one of the most efficient in the world. Fifty cameras observe the city's 'vulnerable' points day and night. In addition there are 450 police officers (reputed to form the most handsome police force in the world) with modern equipment, supported by a further 200 civilian security officers. In Monaco there is no danger in displaying your wealth, a fact attested by the luxury yachts, expensive automobiles, haute-couture clothing and precious jewellery.

The tiny Princely State includes the old city on the Rock, Monte Carlo, La Condamine, which is the harbour and business district situated between the two, and the new town of Fontvieille, built on reclaimed land and devoted mostly to business, but also the site of an impressive modern sports stadium.

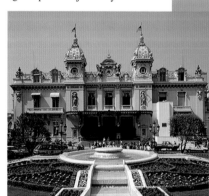

Taking a Tour

This itinerary begins in Monaco, the capital of this miniature state, which is built on the 300-metre (1,000-ft) wide and 800-metre (2,600-ft) long cliff known as the Rock, extending out to sea. In the **Cathedral** there are several altar paintings by Louis Bréa. Princess Grace is buried here. In the alleyways of the Old City you can often hear 'Les Petits Chanteurs de Monaco' on Sunday mornings, as they sing mass in the Cathedral.

The **Placette Bosio** commemorates the poet Guillaume Apollinaire, who used to walk through the shady alleys of the **Jardin St Martin**. The members

Left: Monaco, home to the rich and famous
Above: Louis Bréa's altarpiece in the cathedral. **Above right**: the Casino

of the Grimaldi dynasty are immortalised as wax-work figures in the **Musée de Cires** (27 Rue Basse, tel: 377-93 30 39 05; 10am–6pm daily, Apr–June and Sep–Dec; 10am–7pm July and Aug; 11am–5pm Jan–Mar), on one of the most picturesque steets in the old quarter.

Tthe **Musée Océanographique** (Avenue Saint Martin, tel: 377-93 15 36 00; 9am–7pm daily Aprl–Jun and Sep; 9am–8pm July and Aug; 10am–6pm Oct–Mar) was founded in 1910 by Prince Albert I, whose passion for research took him on many sea voyages; its aquarium has more than 90 tanks.

Continue to the **Place du Palais** in front of the Prince's Palace, which, with its cannons and cannonballs, has something of an operatic air. This impression is strengthened by the changing of the guard (every day at 11.55am). From the parapet on one side of the square there is a fabulous view of the harbour, of Monte Carlo, the coast along to the point of Bordighera, the new quarter of Fontvieille and the Cap d'Ail. In summer it is possible to visit part of the **Palais du Prince** and the **Napoleonic**

Monaco

300 m / 330 yds

Museum, in one wing (tel: 377-93 25 18 31; both open daily, 9.30am–6pm June–Sep, 10am–5pm in Oct; closed Nov–May).

Leaving the Rock by bus, the next stop is the **Jardin Exotique** (Moneghetti, tel: 377-93 30 33 65; daily 9am–6pm or nightfall, or 7pm May–Sep), an amazing feat of gardening on a cliff. The 8,000 species of plants include varieties of cactus from South America, Mexico and Africa. Another green oasis amid the skyscrapers is the **Parc Paysager** with its freshwater lake, and the **Rose Garden**, created by Prince Rainier in memory of Princess Grace.

Monte Carlo

You should then move on to the exclusive, exotic, extravagant world of **Monte Carlo** and the **Place du Casino**, with its immaculate gardens surrounded by the Casino itself flanked on one side by the Hôtel de Paris and on the other by the more recent **Café de Paris**. Lunch at the Café de Paris is definitely *the* thing to do, although, prices being what one would expect in Monte Carlo, you could just make do with a coffee before strolling next-door for a look at the Casino, well worth a visit for its extravagant architecture and decoration. The slot machines are open all day and admission is free, but to really get a feel of the atmosphere you should go into the **Salons Privés** (open from 3 or 4pm). Should you decide to try your luck at the roulette tables, you should hope for better fortune than the 19th-century courtesan La Belle Otéro, who lost everything in a single evening (though she then won back a fortune by gambling the gold buttons on her dress).

The **Salle Garnier**, straight ahead as you enter the Casino, is the elaborate setting for opera, theatre, ballet and concerts, complete with theatre boxes for royalty. Do attend a gala performance if you get the chance, as admiring the outfits of society patrons is entertainment in itself.

Venturing back out of the Casino, shoppers should head for the **Rue Grimaldi** or the **Galérie Metropole** beneath Monte Carlo's deluxe hotel, the **Metropole Palace**. Alternatively, the **Musée Nationale Automates et Poupées d'Autrefois** down by the beach (17 Avenue Princess Grace, tel: 377-93 30 91 26; daily 10am–12.15pm and 2.30–6.30pm, Oct–Easter; 10am–6.30pm Easter–Sep; closed some bank holidays) has a collection of 18th- and 19th-century dolls and automata which are regularly set in motion.

The choice of fine restaurants for dinner in Monte Carlo is huge. My favourite for Italian specialities is **Polpetta**, or for a real splash you could dine in style at the Louis XV in the Hôtel de Paris. Entertainment is also plentiful; for bars with atmosphere try the **La Rascasse** on Quai Antoine. The Casino stages a cabaret, and the **Monte Carlo Sporting Club** puts on star-studded shows in summer. To dance the night away alongside the jet-set, go to one of the nightclubs such as **Jimmy'z** or the **Living Room**.

Above left: sign for the Musée Océanographique
Right: at the foot of the Jardin Exotique, Fontvieille

4. MENTON – THE LEMON CAPITAL *(see pull-out map)*

Eglise St Michel; Rue St Michel; Palais Carnolès; gardens including the view from the Jardin des Colombières; excursions from Menton.

Allow half a day for exploring Menton, and a full day if you also take one of the recommended excursions

With 300 days of sunshine per year and a backdrop of protective mountains covered in citrus and olive groves, Menton has one of the warmest climates on the Riviera. It also has a casino, nightclubs, marinas and sandy beaches. Determined to make the most of the climate, the city's maxim is to offer its citizens and visitors an impressive array of cultural events: concerts, museums, exhibitions, a theatre season from October to April, the Lemon Festival in February/March, festive evenings in the **Parc du Pian**, a circle

of poets and a Katherine Mansfield literary circle (the New Zealand-born author spent some time in Menton around the turn of the century).

Chamber Music and Cocteau

The well-known Chamber Music Festival, created by the Hungarian André Borocz some 45 years ago, is especially worthy of mention. Borocz's hatred of ants drove him to despair on his holiday in Juan-les-Pins, moving him to take quarters with friends in Menton. Here, on a beautiful August evening, he discovered the Italianate plaza in front of the **Eglise St Michel**; the sound of Haifitz playing a Bach violin concerto drifted out of an open window and created an acoustic backdrop for the sunset. Borocz was moved by this serendipitous weaving of events, and sought to reproduce the experience for others. The intimate *parvi* provides a unique setting for the chamber music festival performances: the ochre of the largest and most beautiful Baroque church in the area, the rose hue of the adjacent chapel, cobblestones arranged into the Grimaldi coat of arms... and a ceiling of glowing stars.

Not far from the Eglise St Michel is the **Town Hall** where the room used to conduct marriage ceremonies is decorated by Jean Cocteau. If you stroll down towards the harbour, you will come to the **Musée Jean Cocteau** (Quai Monléon, tel: 04 93 57 72 30; 10am–noon and 2–6pm); closed Tues and bank holidays) in the little 17th-century fort. Behind St Michael's church, the Rue Longue follows the Via Julia Augusta, the former main traffic artery and a route originally laid by the Romans. The **Rue St Michel** with its orange trees is a popular pedestrian shopping zone; below it is the delightful **Place aux Herbes** and the covered market, next to the **Place du Marché** with its flower stalls.

At the west end of the town is the 18th-century **Palais Carnolès**, the former summer residence of the Monaco royal family. This attractive pink and white palace is set in a beautiful park and looks very Italian; the abundant art collection in its **Musée des Beaux Arts** (3 Avenue de la Madone, tel:

Above: one of Menton's beaches. **Above right**: exhibit in the Musée Jean Cocteau
Right: Eze, a classic *village perché*

04 93 35 49 71; 10am–noon and 2–6pm; closed Tues and bank holidays) is worth a visit.

Aubrey Beardsley

Menton is famous for its many gardens. The **Jardin Biovès** was built right over the Careï River. With its tall palms, citrus trees, fountains and statues, the garden is the centre of February's Lemon Festival. Up above the church the old cemetery – where the artist Aubrey Beardsley is buried – affords some of the best views of town and sea. Another beautiful view over the rising arcades of Old Menton can be enjoyed from the private **Jardin des Colombières** (Rue Ferdinand Bac, tel: 04 92 10 33 66; open on 40 days each year, normally July and heritage days), laid out by the author and architect Ferdinand Bac. The **Jardin Botanique Val Rahmeh** (Avenue St Jacques, tel: 04 93 35 86 72; 10am–12.30pm and 2–5pm, or 3–6pm April–Sep) contains some 700 species of Mediterranean and tropical flora.

There are numerous possible outings from Menton: to **Gorbio** (D23) or **St Agnès** (D22), two attractive mountain villages with wonderful views of the coast; the **Annonciade Monastery** (D2566), a destination for pilgrims since the 11th century; the Forest of Menton, a pleasant place for hiking; or up towards **Sospel** beyond the **Col de Castillon**. On market day (Friday) you may like to visit the Italian town of **Ventimiglia** just over the border.

5. EZE AND CAP MARTIN *(see map, p28)*

Eze Village; the ruins of the Saracen fortress with a view over the entire Riviera; dining in the Château Eza or in the Chèvre d'Or; the exclusive residential area of Cap Martin on the Peninsula.

This half day tour takes the fast N7 (Moyenne Corniche) between Nice and Menton, a distance of 31km (20 miles)

The broad, much-improved N7 is the fastest route from Nice to **Eze Village**. To get up into the village, join the throng passing through the gate of the old

Saracen fortress on the Avenue du Jardin Exotique and on up the Rue du Brec to the church with its Baroque interior. Then follow the Rue de la Paix and the Rue du Château with its archways, and climb the steps to the **Jardin Exotique** (tel: 04 93 41 10 30; daily 9am–5pm, till 7.45pm in summer).

There is little left of the castle, destroyed on the orders of Louis XIV, but at this point you are 429 metres (1,407ft) above sea-level with a sweeping view across the Riviera. On the way down stop to admire the 14th-century **Chapelle des Pénitents Blancs**, whose outside walls are decorated with enamel paintings. At the end of the Rue de la Pise is the Moorish gateway on your right, and on your left the former residence of Prince William of Sweden. Now a hotel and restaurant, the **Château Eza** (*see Practical Information, page 88*) will satisfy the most demanding of clientele. The **Chèvre d'Or** (*see Eating Out*) is a second gourmet temple in the Rue du Barri. If you want to stop for lunch in one of them (expensive but worth it), you must reserve.

To Cap Martin

Past Eze, the Moyenne Corniche continues around the Tête de Chien and then passes above the Principality of Monaco (*see Monaco Itinerary, page 30*). Remaining on the same road, you will arrive in **Beausoleil**, which nestles in the south cliffs of the Mont des Mules. After that the Corniche leads on past the Vista Palace Hotel and joins the coastal road just east of **Roque-**

brune, a town which is divided into two parts: a modern seaside resort and an old village (*see Grande Corniche Itinerary, opposite*).

Continuing east of Roquebrune, you will come to **Cap Martin**, Menton's most exclusive neighbourhood. This peninsula is lush with olive groves, cypresses, mimosas and pine woods, among which are some splendid hidden villas and grounds, whose owners are no doubt very happy that there is nothing else in this area to attract tourists.

The mild climate and flourishing vegetation have long appealed to those with the means of living here: the beautiful Sissi of Austria loved the south and the sea; the French Empress Eugénie hoped for an improvement in her illness while staying here; King Umberto of Italy, Sir Winston Churchill, Le Corbusier and Coco Chanel came here for the peace and quiet.

The 'immortal' Greta Garbo, always on the run from the public eye, hid here in the splendidly located estate of the Russian Princess Anna Chervachidzé, which today belongs to the Lebanese billionaire Hani Salaam. Silvano Mangano and the Italian film producer Dino de Laurentiis have frequently tarried here in the residence Casa del Mare. So be on the lookout for well-known current residents and visitors – although, of course, recognising celebrities in the flesh is not always easy.

Above: souvenir shop in Eze

6. THE GRAND CORNICHE *(see map, p28)*

From Nice to Roquebrune via the Grande Corniche: La Turbie and the Trophée des Alpes; Roquebrune village.

This half day tour takes the Grande Corniche east from Nice

Napoleon ordered the construction of this uppermost Corniche, which partly follows the course of the Roman Aurelian Way. Leaving Nice you pass the **Observatory** (Boulevard de l'Observatoire, tel: 04 92 00 30 11; open Sat 3–4.30pm), designed by Charles Garnier and Gustave Eiffel. Shortly before the **Col des 4-Chemins** you come to the entrance to the **Paillon Valley**, and through the opening you can see straight up to the Alps. Just past here, the **Ferme St Michel** (tel: 04 93 76 68 38, open evening only, daily except Tues Jun–Sep; Sun lunch only Oct–May) offers a full menu in a lovely location.

Alternatively, as you pass the **Col d'Eze** a little further on, the Plateau de la Justice by the Hôtel Hermitage is a good place for a picnic. From the Col d'Eze (508m/1,665ft), there is a view north towards the upper Var and Vésubie valleys, and a hiking path that leads into the **Parc de la Révère**. The **Trophée des Alpes (Alpine Trophy)** is a 35-metre (115-ft) high restored Roman victory monument, originally topped by a statue of Augustus Caesar. The Trophy gave the nearby settlement its name: Tropea Augusti, now **La Turbie**. The Rue Comte de Cessol, formerly Via Julia, leads past medieval houses up to the monument, where there's also a museum (tel: 04 93 41 20 84; museum and Trophy open 9.30am–7pm, July–Sep; 10am–5pm, Oct–Mar, closed Mon; 9.30am–6pm April–June; closed some bank holidays).

To Cap Martin

The road continues down to **Roquebrune**, France's only preserved settlement dating from the Carolingian period (AD742–814). The name of the village comes from the reddish-brown cliffs into which it was built. Stroll through the steep covered streets and climb the ancient staircases up to the 13th-century keep. For over 500 years a procession has been held on 5 August in Roquebrune to commemorate one held in 1467, said to have prevented a plague epidemic. Today on this date villagers re-enact scenes from the Passion. Just outside the village, on the Chemin de Menton, is a 1,000-year-old olive tree.

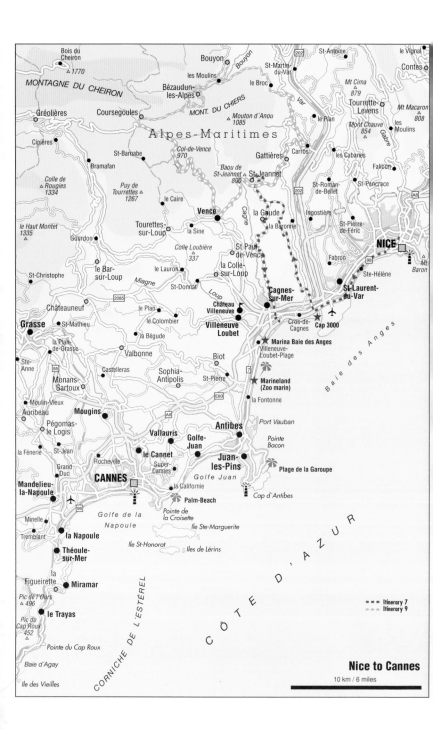

Nice to Cannes

10 km / 6 miles

Itinerary 7
Itinerary 9

7. ST LAURENT AND HAUT-DE-CAGNES *(see map, p38)*

The yacht harbour of St Laurent; La Gaude; Haut-de-Cagnes and its castle; the Musée Renoir.

Leave Nice on the Promenade des Anglais, heading west. This tour covers a distance of 22km (14 miles); allow a good half day

Until 1860, when the County of Nice fell to France, the River Var represented the border between France and the Kingdom of Sardinia. The town of **St Laurent-du-Var** was in charge of the river crossing. Travellers from Paris to Nice, who had spent 12 uncomfortable days in their coaches, were carried on the shoulders of two strong men over the ford of the torrential mountain river. Today the crossing is much easier with three major roads bridging the now somewhat tamer river. St Laurent yachting harbour is a pleasant place for a stroll, with a wide choice of restaurants should it be getting on for mealtime. **Sant 'Ana** *(see page 80)* is good for seafood.

High and Low

If you are ready to get away from the hubbub of the coast, a good evasive move is to take the Corniche du Var (D118). This road, providing beautiful views of the hinterlands of Nice, leads past the IBM Research Centre to **La Gaude** (turn left on to the D18) where the writer Marcel Pagnol spent some time. Now you have a pleasant choice: from La Gaude you can either drive on to **St Jeannet**, near Vence, passing along the way a 14th-century castle originally owned by the Knights Templar, or you can continue down to the coast via the hill-top village of **Haut-de-Cagnes**, which is well worth a side-trip of its own.

If you decide in favour of the latter, as you come down into the town of Cagnes-sur-Mer, follow signs right to the Haut-de-Cagnes. The best places to park are either in the underground multi-storey garage built into the mountain, where your car is taken down by lift, or anywhere you can find room on the street on your way up to the castle. The only way to see the old village is on foot; every corner hides attractive houses, tiny flower-filled squares, alleyways and arched passages. The fortress was originally built by Rainier Grimaldi, Lord of Monaco and Admiral of France, after he became Lord of Cagnes in 1309.

The *Cagnois* who sheltered within its walls cultivated wheat, vines and olives on the surrounding hills. These staples, along with fish landed at the harbour of Cros-de-Cagnes, were brought up into the village on mules.

In the 17th century Henri Grimaldi had the 300-year-old citadel remodelled into

Right: inside the Château Grimaldi, Haut-de-Cagnes

a magnificently appointed castle. But with the coming of the French Revolution this feudal mode of life came to an abrupt halt, ending an era of luxury. The then Lord of Monaco, Gaspard Grimaldi, was forced to leave Cagnes and abandon his castle. He fled to Nice, a duchy which in those days still belonged to the counts of Savoy. **St Peter's Church**, located beneath the Porte de Nice,which has an attractive wrought-iron bell tower of the sort commonly seen in Provence, contains the tombs of the Grimaldis of Cagnes.

The **Château Grimaldi** remained unoccupied until a buyer was finally found in the 19th century. It has belonged to the city of Cagnes-sur-Mer since 1939. Today the Château-Musée (tel: 04 92 02 47 30;10am–noon and 2–5pm, or 6pm May–Sep; closed Tues and some bank holidays) incorporates several interesting museums: the **Musée Ethnographique de l'Olivier**, where you can learn everything there is to know about the olive; the **Musée d'Art Moderne Méditerranéen**; and the **Suzy Solidor collection**. The latter is especially interesting for its portraits of Suzy, a 1930s Parisian nightclub singer, painted by some 40 significant 20th-century artists.

Remembering Renoir

Haut-de-Cagnes has long been connected with modern painting: a number of German artists worked here in the 1930s, and since 1969 the castle has hosted the annual **Festival International de la Peinture** during the summer. Auguste Renoir (1841–1919) is without doubt Cagnes' most famous painter. Towards the end of the 19th century, suffering from a painful attack of gout, Renoir moved to the South of France on the advice of his doctor. In Cagnes he found all the ingredients he was looking for: a hilly, idyllic landscape, a favourable microclimate that would be beneficial to his health and, above all, wonderful light for his work. It was always the light that fascinated Renoir, as it was for his friends Monet and Sisley. He worked in the open air, concentrating on the challenge of portraying sunlight and its reflections on canvas.

In 1903 Renoir established himself in the Maison de la Poste, which now serves as the town hall. In 1907, he acquired, on the advice of his friend who later became mayor of Cagnes, **Les Collettes**, a plot of land with ancient olive trees. Here he built the house in which he spent the last 12 years of his life. In 1960 the city of Cagnes bought the villa and turned it into the **Musée Renoir** (19 Chemin des Colettes, tel: 04 92 02 47 30; 10am–noon and 2–5pm, or 6pm May–Sep; closed Tues and some bank holidays). Everything was left in its original condition and it is easy to feel transported back to the time when Renoir spent hours before the easel in the shade of his olive trees. Works by Bonnard and Dufy are also on display.

You can dine very well in Cagnes, either at **Les Peintres**, a restaurant famed for its delectable lobster, or **JosyJo**, another excellent choice. From Cagnes it is only a short distance on to Vence, the next major destination in this book.

Left: Venus, Musée Renoir

8. VENCE – CITY OF ARTISTS *(see map, p43)*

In and around the medieval hilltop town of Vence: Place du Peyra; the Forum of the old Roman town; the medieval town and Cathedral; Provençal cuisine in the Auberge des Seigneurs or at Maximin.

The distance from Nice to Vence is 22km (14 miles); allow half a day

Vence is only 10km (6 miles) away from the coast, and yet it gives visitors the impression of a completely different world. The locals proudly boast: 'Provence begins in Vence', and Mistral, the famous poet of this region, writing in dialect, said: *'Desempiei Arle jusquá Venco – Escoutas me Gént de Prouvenco,'* which roughly translates as, 'From Arles to Vence the people speak Provençal.'

Those who have seen Chagall's painting *The Lovers of Vence* will be surprised by the approaches to the city, since the modern Vence outside the old walls, with its horrible new buildings, in no way resembles the *village perché* depicted in the work of this poetic artist. However, the picturesque old Vence at the foot of the Baous mountains, which protect it from the cold north winds, has remained unchanged, having preserved its typically Provençal character especially well.

Roman Spa

The medieval core of the city, surrounded by an elliptical wall with five gates, makes it rather difficult for the visitor to imagine the Roman city of Vintium. In those days Vence was already a popular health resort owing to its mild climate, and the water from the **Source de la Foux** was just as popular for its health benefits then as now.

Entering the city through the **Porte Peyra** you come to the **Place du Peyra**, the Forum of the old Roman city, where ancient chestnut trees shade the cafés. The beautiful urn-shaped fountain here dates from 1822. Continue along the **Rue du Marché**, a colourful, narrow market street where meat, fish, cheese, wine, fresh pasta, fruit and vegetables are sold, to arrive at the **Place Clemenceau** on your left, the site of a flea market every Tuesday. The Town Hall is located here on the site of the former bishop's palace.

Above: Vence market

In 374, shortly after its conversion by the monks of St Honorat, Vence became an episcopal city, starting quite a tradition of venerable clerics. The bishops St Véran (5th century) and St Lambert (12th century) were declared saints; Farnese (16th century) declined the Vence bishop's crosier, going instead to the Holy See to become Pope Paul III. He proved to be quite generous to Vence, however, and donated several reliquaries.

Bishop Godeau was an enthusiastic visitor to the Hôtel des Rambouillet, which was then a centre of literary life, and he was made the first member of the Académie Française by Richelieu. Bishop Surian (18th century) parted with his fortune for the benefit of a hospital.

Vence's loss of rank as a bishop's see in 1801 can be traced to Napoleon and the Pope. At first the honour passed to Fréjus, then, in 1860, it went to the diocese of Nice when the right bank of the Var became permanently French.

Cathedral Treasures

On the site of the **Cathedral** there once stood a temple to Mars, and later a Merovingian church. As a result of the repeated alteration and expansion of the original Roman building, the present structure is a peculiar mixture of styles. Throughout the cathedral are exquisite examples of Carolingian carving incorporated in the walls and columns, which were from the previous church.

The two side aisles were roofed over in the 15th century by a wide gallery which looks down into the nave through a row of arches, built to accommodate an enlarged congregation. Either side are two more aisles, which contain the chapels. Inside these you will find the tombs of saints Véran and Lambert. There is a mosaic of Moses in the bullrushes, designed by Chagall, in the Baptistry, and a choir pew of 51 stalls made of oak and pear-tree wood which was designed by Jacques Bellot of Grasse in the 15th century. Despite the 25 years of work that went into making the pew, it is evident from the detail that he did not lose his sense of humour. He carved animals and plants and recorded the everyday life of the people and clergy, sometimes not at all reverently.

From the **Place Godeau**, with a granite Roman column in the centre, you have a good view of the rectangular tower, a Renaissance door from 1575, courtyards and alleyways, as well as a picturesque corner which goes by the name of L'Enfer (Hell).

Continue along Rue St Lambert and then Rue de l'Hôtel de Ville to reach the **Porte du Signadour**. Directly opposite the gate is a 15th-century fountain. If you turn left you pass the **Porte de l'Orient**, for which you

Above: Vence cathedral
Left: menu with an artistic touch

once needed to have your own key. The date recorded up on the left of the gate commemorates the time when the Huguenots attempted, unsuccessfully, to lay siege to the city.

The old Alphonse Toreille Seminary, constructed by Godeau in 1669, is located a short walking distance from here. The **Boulevard Paul André** leads along the city wall, large sections of which are still preserved. The view of the Baous and the outer spurs of the Alps is beautiful here.

Place du Frêne

Now return to the Place du Peyra by way of **Portail Lévis** and **Rue du Portail Lévis**. The **Château Seigneurial**, built by Villeneuve in the 16th century (also known as Château Villeneuve), is located on the **Place du Frêne**. Today it houses the **Fondation Emile Hugues**, a centre of modern and contemporary art (tel: 04 93 58 15 78; 10am–6pm July–Sep; 10am–12.30pm and 2–6pm Oct–June; closed Mon and some bank holidays). The old **ash tree** on the plaza in front of the château is supposed to have been planted in the 16th century, in honour of Franz I and Pope Paul III. The restaurant **Auberge des Seigneurs** serves Provençal dishes in a dining room with a large, beautiful fireplace. According to rumour, it lost its star because clandestine visitors representing the Michelin guides were served a dessert in the shape of a penis.

Many writers and artists were attracted to Vence after World War I. Among them André Gide, Paul Valéry, Chaim Soutine and Raoul Dufy all made extended visits. In 1955, when the city had only 6,000 inhabitants, a new generation of artists came to Vence: Céline, Tzara, Cocteau, Matisse, Chagall, Carzou and Dubuffet. Today Vence has a population of 17,000, and its artistic tradition continues. Arman, born in Nice, has been an American citizen since 1972, but every year he leaves New York to return to Vence. His house, which originally looked like an overturned, half-buried boat, now resembles a work of art. A wing added in 1980 features 2,300 wash-tubs.

Vence is not just an attractive vacation town, it's also a good starting point for excursions into the splendid hinterland (*see Around Vence, page 44*).

And Vence is a splendid place to eat. The Auberge des Seigneurs has already been mentioned; it's rivalled now by the restaurant established here more recently by the legendary Jacques Maximin and perhaps *the* best place to sample the 'cuisine du soleil' (*see Restaurants, page 81, for details*).

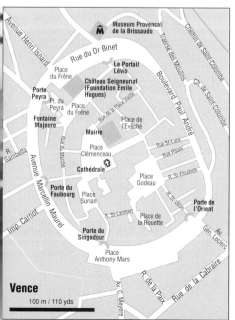

Vence

100 m / 110 yds

9. VILLAGES AROUND VENCE *(see maps, p38)*

The Rosary Chapel decorated by Matisse; the Baous; lunch in St Jeannet; the pretty mountain villages of Gattières and Le Broc; horse-riding at Ranch El Bronco; the Col de Vence

This excursion from Vence covers a distance of 60km (38 miles); allow a whole day to cover everything included here

The historic and picturesque villages around Vence, many of them largely undisturbed by mass tourism, are well worth exploring, as is the beautiful mountainous countryside. For years these characterful villages were very isolated, connected to larger towns only by a few mule tracks.

As you leave Vence heading northeast towards St Jeannet on the D2210, you have to watch carefully to avoid driving straight past the Provençal building with a glazed cross on its roof. Matisse was 80 when he designed and decorated the **Chapelle du Rosaire**, 1947–51 (Avenue Henri Matisse, tel: 04 93 58 03 26; 10–11.30am and 2.30–5.30pm Tues and Thur, also 2.30–5.30pm Wed, Fri and Sat 6 July–31 Aug; closed public holidays).

Setting off again on the same road, pull over into the first lay-by to look back at the fully intact city wall surrounding Vence. As you do so, you will also discover a viaduct, a vestige of the days when you could ride on the single track railway from Nice to Draguignan. The tunnels for this railway line, destroyed by the Resistance during World War II, serve today for cultivating mushrooms. Continuing your drive you can already make out the imposing south face of the **Baou of St Jeannet**. Mountaineers come from all over the world to climb its sheer face, towering 400m (1,300ft) above the village and with some 35 different possible ascents. With suitable shoes it is not difficult to hike to the summit, from which there is a spectacular panoramic view. Allow an hour each way to do it comfortably.

Italian Influence

After the exercise you may be ready for a good lunch at the **Auberge St Barbe**. Specialities are stuffed sardines, *petit niçoise farcie* (stuffed tomatoes, onions and courgettes), *ravioli aux cèpes* (pasta parcels with mushrooms – showing the Italian influence on cuisine in this area) and steamed salmon. **St Jeannet** is one of the few villages withing easy striking distance of the

coast to have retained its authenticity; here the tourists tend to be climbers and hikers and you will find local *épiceries* and *boulangeries* rather than arts and crafts workshops.

The next stop is **Gattières**, a maze of picturesque alleyways offering wonderful views of the Alps. It is hard to imagine that winter sports are available for much of the year on the snow-capped peaks little more than an hour's drive away, in the resorts of Isola 2000, Auron and Valberg.

Along the Var

You should now branch off the D2210 onto the D2209, which follows the River Var, to the old village of **Carros**. Its attractive houses are marshalled around a castle on the top of a hill; a little below them, next to an old mill, there is an observation platform with a panoramic view. The 'new' Carros stretched below is rather less attractive. From here on the villages get smaller, quieter and more untouched.

Le Broc (*broco* means olive-cutting) was quite popular with a number of bishops who sought relaxation here. This splendidly located village possesses an idyllic plaza with arcaded buildings. There is also a fountain whose cool waters have been the salvation of hikers arriving via the mountain from St Jeannet. **Bouyon**, once a border village between Nice and Savoy, has little over 200 residents now , mostly senior citizens, and a number of the houses around the rectangular village plaza are for sale. The view is fantastic over the Cheiron, the Var and Esteron valleys and the Alps of the Italian border region.

Now take the D8 through ever more wild and deserted countryside along the Chiers mountain range, to arrive at **Bezaudun-les-Alpes**, remarkable for its houses' fabulous old doors. Above the gorge of the River Cagne, the tall façades of the houses of **Coursegoules** seem to reach for the sky. If the church door is unlocked, you should spend a couple of minutes admiring the panels painted by the omnipresent local artist Louis Bréa.

Drive back to Vence on the D2, situated high above the River Cagne, which swells during periods of heavy rain, creating some beautiful water-falls. The road passes the **Ranch El Bronco** (tel: 04 93 58 09 83) where horse-riders can set out, with a guide, through the spartan but charming thyme-scented landscape.

Just past the **Col-de-Vence** (altitude 1,128m/3,700ft), drive as slowly as possible to admire the view. From here you can see the whole mountain chain between the right bank of the Var and Mont Agel, and the coast from Cap Ferrat, past Nice and the Baie des Anges, the Antibes peninsula, the islands off Cannes, and right along to the Esterel.

Left: St Jeannet
Above: a cyclist along the Var

10. ST PAUL *(see map, p38)*

St Paul, a traditional artists' colony: handicrafts in the Rue Grande, the famous Colombe d'Or restaurant; the Fondation Maeght; antiques in La Colle-sur-Loup; the horse-racing track in Cagnes-sur-Mer.

St Paul is 20km (12 miles) from Nice and 5km (3 miles) from Vence. Allow half a day

Gently rolling hills and fertile valleys, which have unfortunately become densely settled, surround the hill on which perches **St Paul-de-Vence**, a village originally built as a border fortification in the 16th century. In the 1920s St Paul was discovered by painters like Signac, Bonnard, Modigliani and Soutine. These young and as yet unknown artists lodged in the modest *auberge* at the entrance to the village, where they were able to pay with their paintings. The word got around quickly, and Derain, Utrillo, Vlaminck and Matisse came too, followed by young intellectuals such as Prévert, Camus, Giono, Maeterlinck, Morand and Kipling, who transformed the village into a sort of St-Germain-des-Près-de-la-Mer. In the 1940s people from the cinema industry joined the party. Today it is difficult to imagine the peace and quiet of this once so typical Provençal village, especially as it is now one of the most popular tourist destinations in France.

Only residents are allowed to drive into St Paul, and even then they are limited to the road running round the edge. Leave your car well outside, and stroll along the **Rue Grande**, the narrow cobble-stoned main street which cuts through the length of the village. In the almost too perfectly restored old streets and houses, decorated with their coats of arms, you will find endless arts and crafts shops and galleries. You should get up early if you want to enjoy the atmosphere undisturbed by the multilingual chattering of the crowds as they pile out of their coaches later in the day. You will be glad you made the effort as you admire the little square with the urn-shaped fountain and the vaulted washing-house, glimpse in-

Above: St Paul
Left: sculpture at Fondation Maeght

side a church, spend a couple of minutes at **Chagall's grave** and make your way back along the village wall, past wonderful gardens hidden behind high walls and full of orange trees, to the **Café de la Place**, where you can get an especially good *café crême* and skim the pages of *Nice Matin* (the local newspaper). In front of the café you will undoubtedly see the locals playing *boules*, which is a passion for many of them.

Many of the well-known figures associated with St Paul are sadly no longer there: Lino Ventura, James Baldwin, Chagall, Kurt Jürgens, Yves Montand… and La Mère Roux, proprietor of the renowned restaurant the **Colombe d'Or**. A portrait of this white-haired old lady who radiated energy hangs in the bar of the simple *auberge*. Lunch or dinner on the terrace of the Colombe d'Or is still one of the Côte d'Azur's truly magic experiences. Be sure to reserve a table, and sample the 15 *hors d'oeuvres*, leaving room for the main course and the Grand Marnier soufflé for dessert. Afterwards stroll through the dining-room with its painted wooden ceiling and walls hung with works by Picasso, Miro, Dufy, Chagall, Matisse, and out to the garden where a huge mosaic by Léger adorns the wall, alongside a Calder mobile.

Memorable Modern Art

A visit to the **Fondation Maeght**, just a short walk from St Paul (tel: 04 93 32 81 63; 10am–12.30pm and 2.30–6pm daily, 10am–7pm July–Sep) is an absolute must. To get there, go down the main road from the village towards La Colle-sur-Loup and take the first turning right.

Art dealers Aimé and Marguerite Maeght created this beautiful and lively museum of modern art with the help of architect José Luis Sert. The two main buildings joined by an entrance hall are constructed in a light-coloured concrete and red brick, and adorned with a basin-like roof design which is reminiscent of a Mediterranean rain storage tank. In addition to the museum's own considerable collection, major exhibitions based on a particular theme or the work of a contemporary painter are held each year. There is also a bookshop, library and cafeteria. The museum's landscaped gardens contain a gigantic sculpture by Calder, a variety of mobiles, a fountain with moving metal cylinders, as well as other sculptures and ceramics by Miró and Giacometti, among others.

Leaving St Paul, drive back down to Cagnes-sur-Mer via **La Colle-sur-Loup**, whose street is packed with antique shops, which you may want to browse through. When you arrive in Cagnes-sur-Mer drive down to the coast and turn right towards Antibes. On the right-hand side is the **Hippodrome de la Côte d'Azur**, the Riviera's famous horse-racing track (racing mid-Dec–mid-Mar in daylight hours, and on the cooler evenings July and Aug).

Further along the coast you can't help but notice the controversial modern architecture of the pyramid-shaped **Marina Baie des Anges**, a luxury apartment and yacht harbour complex, visible from many kilometres away.

Right: playing *boules*

11. VILLENEUVE-LOUBET AND VALBONNE *(see map, p38)*

Villeneuve-Loubet: the medieval château and the Musée d'Art Culinaire; continue to Valbonne and Sophia Antipolis High Technology Park; Marineland; the Siesta.

Villeneuve-Loubet is 16km (10 miles) from Nice. The continuation to Valbonne is a further15km (9 miles). Allow a full day

There is a good view of the Baie des Anges from the old town of Villeneuve-Loubet. Just off the N7 and only 2km (1¼ miles) from the coast on the left bank of the Loup, it can seem a long way from the crowds. The medieval streets are tucked around the **Château Villeneuve**, built in the 12th century with a 30-metre (100-ft) tower. The Peace Treaty of Nice was signed here in 1538 and the castle was restored in the 19th century. Today it is privately owned and cannot be visited.

The **Musée d'Art Culinaire** (3 Rue Escoffier, tel: 04 93 20 80 51; 2–6pm in winter, 2–7pm in summer; closed Mon, bank holidays and Nov) was founded in 1966 with the aim of establishing a museum of culinary arts in the house in which the 'king of chefs and chef of kings' was born, in recognition of the services which Auguste Escoffier rendered to the world of cuisine. As well as a typical Provençal kitchen and a display of Escoffier's own cooking utensils, the museum includes an exhibition of 15,000 menus, some of which date back to 1820, and an interesting display of cookery books.

The most important meeting of Escoffier's life was with César Ritz, for whom he first worked in 1883 in the Grand Hotel in Monte Carlo. When Ritz took over the Savoy in London, this became the meeting-place for high society, thanks largely to Escoffier. In 1898 Ritz opened the establishment which bears his name in Paris. Again, it was to Escoffier that the hotel owed its immediate success. In 1899 he followed Ritz to London's Carlton, which he did not leave until 1920, when he finally returned to Monte Carlo aged 74. He died on February 12, 1935. He is known for having created the peach melba, but it is perhaps less well-known that he developed the stock cube with Julius Maggi, now a basis for cuisine the world over.

Happy Valley

West of Villeneuve-Loubet, along the bendy N2085 towards Grasse, you enter the 'Vallis bona' (Happy Valley), which has been cultivated since antiquity. Take a left turn along the minor road signed to **Valbonne**. The history of this settlement dates back to the 13th century when the Chalais order founded the monastery which is now the church on the river-bank below the village. The village centre is the beautiful **Place des Arcades**, shaded by old elm trees. The pretty old fountain is worth a look.

Valbonne owes its modern-day importance to senator Pierre Lafitte, the former director of the highly respected Paris School of Engineering. On a wooded plateau southeast of Valbonne, he founded the international **Sophia**

Antipolis Science Park for research and non-polluting industry. Inspired by the American Silicon Valley example, Lafitte declared, 'One day this region will be considered the California of Europe.' It is conveniently located for access to Nice Côte d'Azur International Airport – the second busiest in France – and the A8 motorway that runs along the coast. Since its founding the park has attracted hundreds of national and international companies bringing thousands of French and foreign workers to the area. Indeed, so succesful has it been that hi-tech industries have now overtaken tourism as the biggest earner in the Alpes-Maritimes *département*. With pleasant residential areas close by, top sporting facilities and cultural centres, Sophia Antipolis has plenty to offer its scientists and business workers.

Killer Whales and Roller-Coasters

From the park, cut down to the coast. If you then drive towards Cagnes-sur-Mer on the N7 you will pass **Marineland** (tel: 04 93 33 49 49; daily 10am–6pm, with late opening in summer), which started out as an aquatic zoo with daily shows with dolphins, sea-lions and killer whales. Though this aspect of the attraction is still popular, the complex has grown to include mini-golf, a butterfly jungle, a little farm and an aqua park. Opposite is a huge fairground which is open from late afternoon all summer. Visitors with children will surely not be allowed to sneak past it.

On the beach between Antibes and Marina Baie des Anges you can't miss the **Siesta**, an open-air nightclub with restaurant, casino and seven dance-floors, one of which is in the form of lily leaves in the middle of a pool (definitely for early-on in the evening, although with the steep price of drinks you may well still be in a fit state to rock and roll without fall off even in the early hours).

Left: Musée d'Art Culinaire
Above: looping the loop, Marineland

12. ANTIBES *(see maps, p38 and pull-out)*

The Château Grimaldi and the Musée Picasso; the Cathedral; the covered market on the Cours Masséna; Plage de la Gravette; Port Vauban Yacht Harbour.

Antibes is 22km (14 miles) from Nice and 11km (7 miles) from Cannes. Allow half a day to explore the town

'I paint Antibes, a small fortified city. Entirely in the gleam of the sun, it rises up from the beautiful mountains and the eternally snow-covered ranges of the

Alps. One ought to paint it with gold and precious gems.' These are the enthusiastic words of Claude Monet, who resided in **Antibes** in 1888. However, in contrast to the paintings Picasso left to the city under the condition that they could never be lent out, the 36 paintings Monet produced here are now in the United States.

The Greek city of Antipolis (Antibes) was founded at the same time as Nikaia (Nice). The city fell into the possession of King Henry IV at the end of the 14th century, when, realising its strategic importance on the border of France and Savoy, he began fortification work which was finally completed in the 17th century by Vauban. Today the ramparts that form the sea-wall and the **Fort Carré** are all that is left. The view from the fortified walls is spectacular, although it is questionable whether Napoleon would have appreciated it when he was held as a prisoner in the Fort Carré after the fall of Robespierre. Painters and writers fleeing Hitler were also interned in the fort.

Château Grimaldi and the Musée Picasso

The **Château Grimaldi** was constructed in the 12th century, in the design of an ancient Roman fort. The rectangular tower, battlements and several window openings are all that remain from that period, however, as the rest of the château was rebuilt in the 16th century. It is open to the public as an art museum, and in the chapel you can see the earliest known illustration of the town of Antibes in the background of a 1539 painting by Antoine Aundi. There are works by Germaine Richier, César, Miró and Pagès on the garden terrace which faces the sea, and Arman's predilection for stringed instruments is admirably documented in the interior courtyard.

The main attraction, however, is the **Musée Picasso**, which is housed in the château (tel: 04 92 90 54 20; 10am–6pm; closed noon–2pm Oct–May, Mon and bank holidays year-round). Here you get a tangible sense of the *joie de vivre* and serenity Picasso must have felt during his stay here in 1946. The war was finally over, there was the splendid studio, provided by the director of the local museum, the sun and light of the south, a new 'young' love (Françoise Gilot, whose book I recommend), renewed fatherhood and the company of good friends such as Prévert and Eluard.

Above: Provençal fisherman
Right: yachts galore

In addition to Picasso's work the museum possesses a collection of contemporary works by Léger, Magnelli, Hartung and Max Ernst as well as the Russian-French painter Nicolas de Staël. The latter lived in Antibes for some time and is said to have plunged to his death from his terrace in 1955. Just next to the Musée Picasso is the Romanesque **Cathedral**.

Those interested in history may like to visit the **Musée d'Histoire et d'Archéologie** (tel: 04 92 90 54 35; 10am–noon and 2–6pm; Oct–May 10am–6pm; closed Mon and bank holidays) in the **Bastion St André** constructed by Vauban. Here you can see finds from Antibes and the surrounding area, discovered during excavations on land and at sea.

The Taste of Provence

The **covered market** (daily except Mon) on the **Cours Masséna** is filled with all the delightful colours, tastes and smells of Provence. If you walk down from here towards the port, you will come to another little square where a flea market is held every Saturday. The **Musée Peynet** (tel: 04 92 90 54 30; 10am–noon and 2–6pm, Oct–May; 10am–6pm June–Sep; closed Mon and some bank holidays), located on the **Place Nationale**, has drawings of Raymond Peynet's cartoon *Lovers* which are known virtually the world over. You can relax at a café or restaurant terrace under the shade of the plane trees and you might even hear floating out of a window a recording by Sidney Bechet, the famous composer and clarinet player, who is buried here.

Around the covered market and along the road continuing down towards the port, there are many cafés and bars with an almost exclusively English clientele. As you reach the port, turn right under the arch and right again through a hole in the harbour wall to the **Plage de la Gravette**, a fine sandy beach.

Antibes has two yacht harbours with over 1,700 berths. The most magnificent luxury yachts – akin to floating palaces – are moored in the modern **Port Vauban Yacht Harbour**, located near the harbour offices. George Nicholson, one of the best-known shipbuilders, knows the yachts, their owners, and their histories. George will tell you that Adnan Kashoggi, for example, owner of the *Nabila*, really loved the sea and spent six months a year on his yacht. Donald Trump bought the *Nabila* from Kashoggi and renamed it *Princess Trump*. When he found out that it wasn't the largest yacht in the world, he came unhappily to Nicholson: 'Could you lengthen it for me?' The yacht was lengthened, but then Trump lost his fortune and his boat. Now owned by a Saudi Prince and renamed Kingdom 5KR, she is still berthed in Antibes.

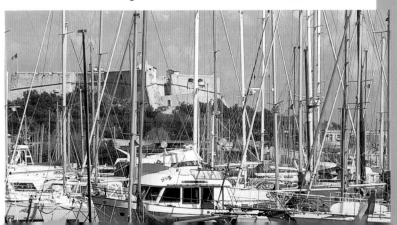

13. CAP D'ANTIBES *(see maps, p38 and pull-out)*

Cap d'Antibes; the Restaurant du Bacon and Hôtel du Cap; the popular holiday town of Juan-les-Pins; Golfe-Juan.

A leisurely tour of the peninsula, roughly 10km/6 miles, takes two hours. If you add Juan-les-Pins and Golfe-Juan allow half a day

The gorgeous **Cap d'Antibes** lies between Antibes and Juan-les-Pins. On the Antibes side, the **Salis** beach affords swimmers a splendid view of the old town of Antibes backed by the Alps. A drive, or better still, a walk, around the Cap is well worthwhile. The Tirpoil pathway has been specially marked out for hikers. Here and there between the famous luxury hotels and villas you can see large greenhouses, mostly growing carnations, small Provençal country houses and even a children's summer camp.

The **Restaurant du Bacon** is known for its excellent fish dishes. A footpath leads up from the coast to the highest point on the Cap. From here you can see from the Esterel to the Alps, and there is a lighthouse whose beams reach my bedroom in Vence. The **Plage de la Garoupe** is set on a very pretty bay, but it is almost impossible to get to the beach itself for all the private restaurants and their sun loungers. Behind the beach is the lovely **Jardin Thuret** (8am–6pm, June–Sep; 8.30am–5.30pm Oct–May; closed Sat and Sun), where some of the first eucalyptus trees to be introduced to Europe were brought from Australia and planted here during the middle of the 19th century.

Exclusive Hideaway

Continuing round the Cap, right out on the southern point is the exclusive **Hôtel du Cap**, whose illustrious guests of the 1920s introduced the summer season to the Riviera. The hotel continues to attract famous guests today, especially during the Cannes Film Festival. Anthony Quinn, Lauren Bacall, Sylvester Stallone and Madonna are just a few of the stars who have spent nights here.

Above: Golfe-Juan promenade

A little further on you come to the **Musée Naval et Napoléonien** (Batterie du Grillon, Avenue J. Kennedy, tel: 04 93 61 45 32; 10am–noon and 2–6pm; closed Sat afternoon, Sun and bank holidays), which awakens memories of the French Emperor's landing here after he escaped from Elba.

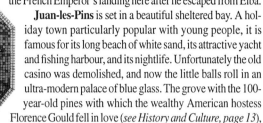

Juan-les-Pins is set in a beautiful sheltered bay. A holiday town particularly popular with young people, it is famous for its long beach of white sand, its attractive yacht and fishing harbour, and its nightlife. Unfortunately the old casino was demolished, and now the little balls roll in an ultra-modern palace of blue glass. The grove with the 100-year-old pines with which the wealthy American hostess Florence Gould fell in love (*see History and Culture, page 13*), creates the setting for an annual open-air **Jazz Festival** featuring many great international names.

The two street-cafés, **Pam-Pam** and **Le Crystal** are open into the early hours. Night-owls can quench their thirst at these cafés with exotic cocktails before moving on to a club or casino, while steamy Latin American rhythms thunder out of oversized loudspeakers.

Golfe-Juan has a modern harbour for yachts and fishing-boats, a sandy beach (still almost deserted in Picasso's time), as well as a beautiful view over to the Lérins Islands and the Cap d'Antibes. On the beach over on the west side of town is **Tétou**, the chic, though pricey, place to go for *bouillabaisse*.

14. VALLAURIS *(see map, p38)*

Vallauris, the 'Ceramic Capital'; Picasso's 'War and Peace' in the Romanesque chapel; Biot.

Vallauris is 31km/20 miles from Nice, 6km (4 miles) from Cannes and 8km (5 miles) from Antibes. Allow two to three hours to explore the town

Vallauris, 2km (1¼ miles) northwest of Golfe-Juan, was already a thriving potter's town in Roman times, on account of the red clay it is built upon. In the 16th century the tradition was continued by Italian potters brought in by the bishop from Grasse. But without the influence of Picasso, Vallauris would certainly not have developed to become known to visitors as the 'Ceramic Capital', as it is today.

Picasso moved to Vallauris in 1947 with the love of his life Françoise Gilot, and they lived in the Villa La Galloise until 1955. It was here that Picasso first turned his hand to pottery, initially working at the Madoura pottery workshop, whose owners, Suzanne and Georges Ramiés, he had met on the beach in Golfe-Juan. His output was tremendous, consisting of over 2,000 pieces during his first year alone.

In 1950 Picasso was made an honorary citizen of the town for his role in saving

Above: Napoleon mosaic
Right: keeping up a Vallauris tradition

its principal industry. He repaid the honour by presenting the town with a life-size bronze statue of a man holding a sheep, which now stands outside the church in the **Place Paul Isnard**. The artist regarded it as an important work: 'I did this statue in a single afternoon, but not until after months of reflection and I don't know how many sketches.'

The **Musée de Vallauris** (Place de la Liberation, tel: 04 93 64 16 05; 10am–noon and 2pm–6pm, or to 5pm, mid-Sep to mid-June; closed Tues and some bank holidays) is in the château, originally a 13th-century priory and rebuilt in the 16th century. All that remains of the original is the Romanesque chapel, which, in 1952, Picasso decorated with his work *War and Peace*. The museum houses lithographs by Picasso, and ceramics designed by the artist and produced by the Galerie Madoura, as well as works by Alberto Magnelli.

The first time I visited France, I also visited Picasso for the first time. I fell in love with both Pablo, the man and artist, and with Vallauris, a romantic little town set on gently rolling hills. My love for Picasso has remained, but not for Vallauris. Françoise Gilot expressed a feeling which I share: 'Pablo's presence brought the town affluence, but his example was not understood. Today Vallauris is a stronghold of bad taste.'

Potters' Shops

Countless ceramic workshops and stores sell huge amounts of kitsch, with pottery shops lining the whole of Rue Clemenceau. The **Galerie Madoura**, owned by the Ramiés' son, is one of the best pottery workshops.

Picasso left Vallauris in 1955. On the occasion of his 90th birthday the town put on a huge folk festival, in which the artist, however, declined to take part. He explained: 'I am helpful for your spectacle, but I don't want to *be* your spectacle.' He watched the festival on television.

Worth visiting nearby (to the northeast) is **Biot**, a village famous for its glassworks and for the **Musée Fernand Léger** (Chemin du Val-de-Pôme, tel: 04 92 91 50 30; 10am–12.30pm and 2–5pm Oct–June; 10.30am–6pm July–Sep; closed Tues and some bank holidays), with a magnificent mosaic on the outside wall.

15. CITY OF CANNES *(see map, p56)*

Belle Epoque buildings; high society, festivals and culinary delights; the Croisette; the Palais des Festivals; the old harbour; seafood at Astoux et Brun; shopping on the Rue d'Antibes.

This full-day tour of Cannes begins on the Croisette

Cannes' reputation for glamour and sophistication is known the world over. In this respect, little has changed in over 100 years. It started in 1834, when Lord Brougham discovered the fishing village by chance. Due to a cholera epidemic, Brougham and his daughter were forced to stay in an *auberge* in the lower Suquet (old town). Brougham was so pleased by its *bouillabaisse*, the harbour, the islands, and the pines and olive groves, that he never arrived in Nice, his original destination, and instead settled in Cannes. For the next 34 years the ex-Chancellor of England wintered in the Villa Eléonore. He started a trend among Europe's aristocracy, which soon turned the Roman harbour of Portus Canuae into an international resort. By 1870 the city already had 35 hotels and 200 villas.

Sumptuous Villas

'Princes, princes, nothing but princes', groaned de Maupassant, who frequently sailed in the bay of La Napoule between 1884 and 1888. 'If you like them, you're in the right place.' In Cannes, the architects of the Belle Epoque had the opportunity to realise their wildest dreams. Sumptuous villas, extravagant palaces and fantastic gardens appeared on the hills of La Californie, La Croix-des-Gardes, Le Cannet and Super-Cannes. The **Villa Alexandra**, with its minarets, could be mistaken for a mosque; **Château Scott** is Gothic in style; the **Villa Camille Amélie** has a natural grotto and huge marble columns; the **Villa Yakimour** was built by the Aga Khan for Yvette Labrousse.

Today Cannes' fame stems largely from its role as a media city, with the Film Festival joined by the TV Festival (MIPTV) and the Record and Music Festival (MIDEM). Around 80,000 visitors come every year for the Film Festival alone. The town's motto is '*La Vie est un Festival*', and there is indeed plenty going on here all year round. Gourmets have come to Cannes to be spoiled in some of the world's greatest restaurants, including the **Carlton**, the **Martinez** and the **Royal Gray**; those looking for something a little less upmarket will also find a restaurant to their taste among over 300 to choose from on the Avenue

Left: pottery kitsch, Vallauris. **Above**: imprint of Sophia Loren. **Right**: one of the world's top hotels

Félix-Faure, around Forville Market, in the Suquet quarter, on the Quai St Pierre and in the streets between the Croisette and the Rue d'Antibes. Everywhere you go there is a wonderful aroma of garlic, truffles, herbs and spices. The local cuisine is, in the words of poet Stéphen Liégeard, '*comme une tranche de soleil sur une nappe de mer bleue*' (like a spot of sunlight on a cloth of blue sea).

Along the Croisette

The **Croisette** must be one of the world's best-known shoreline promenades. Its cosmopolitan nature is attested by the 96 newspapers in 30 different languages that are on sale. This magnificent boulevard, with its majestic palms and elegant, colourful gardens and parks, stretches from **Palm Beach** to the **Palais des Festivals**. Take a stroll along the Croisette, with the sandy beaches on one side decked out in summer with cheerful beach mats and parasols and their restaurants open for lunch. On the other side are luxury boutiques and terrace cafés.

Sit for a while on a bench or chair and admire the palatial hotels, the *monstres sacrés* (holy monsters) of the Belle Epoque: the Carlton, the Majestic and the Martinez, all of which have been completely renovated. The most beautiful is still the Carlton, with its white wedding-cake façade and twin domes which, as the story goes, were inspired by the perfect breasts of La

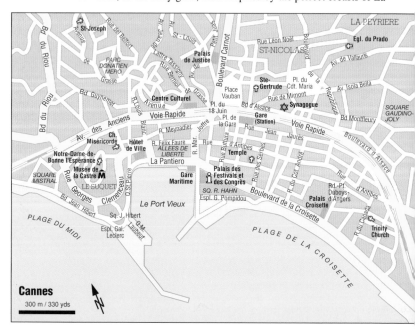

Belle Otéro, a courtesan of the coast at the turn of the century. **La Malmaison** has been turned into a contemporary art gallery (47 La Croisette, tel: 04 93 99 04 04; opening times vary, closed Mon).

The Palais des Festivals, which is where the main events of the Film Festival take place, also houses a casino, a nightclub and cafeteria, and a gigantic underground car park with 950 parking places. Locally known as the 'bunker', the Palais is a modern complex of glass and concrete whose architecture has stimulated some heated debates. In the old harbour beyond it, fishing boats dock alongside luxury yachts.

Opposite the Palais des Festivals are the **Allées de la Liberté**, an attractive place for a stroll and the venue for a colourful flower market in the mornings and a flea market on Saturdays. If you love seafood, you will be spoilt for choice on the Avenue Félix-Faure, but I recommend **Astoux et Brun**, right on the corner at No 27.

A Feast for the Eyes

The city's former main traffic artery, the **Rue Meynadier**, connects the city centre with the **Suquet** quarter, the oldest part of town. It is a lively pedestrian shopping street with outlets selling clothes and food, including a cheese shop, a pasta shop, two butchers and a *traiteur* who have all been awarded medals for the quality of their wares. Forville market (daily except Sundays) is a real feast for the eyes. Not only can you purchase the best fruit, the crispest vegetables and the freshest fish (while rubbing shoulders with Cannes' master-chefs), but you are also taking part in a spectacle which is an integral part of local life.

At the Suquet end of the Rue Meynadier, the **Rue St Antoine**, lined on either side with restaurants, winds its way up to the **Place de la Castre**, on which you will find the **Musée de la Castre** (tel: 04 93 38 55 26; 10am–1pm and 2–5pm, extended hours in summer; closed Mon). This museum contains interesting archaeological collections and art from the Mediterranean, South America and the Pacific. The square tower (22 metres/72ft high) once served as a look-out post. If you walk through the old bell tower you will come to a shady plaza from which you can look out over the whole of Cannes, the harbour and the islands.

Old Cannes is easy to explore, as it consists of only seven or eight little narrow streets grouped around the Suquet. Afterwards, head back towards the centre of town, this time taking the street running parallel to the Croisette, the **Rue d'Antibes**, which is Cannes' main shopping street. Rue d'Antibes is frequently compared to the Rue du Faubourg St-Honoré in Paris, and prices are certainly very similar. What was it Cocteau said? 'One can certainly leave the house without an umbrella, but never without one's wallet – the selection is simply too alluring.'

Left: gone fishing in Cannes
Above: dressed for an occasion

16. GRASSE *(see map, p60)*

In the footsteps of Napoleon; Mougins and its distinguished restaurants; the health-resort town of Grasse, the perfume metropolis, its Cathedral and the Villa-Musée Fragonard; back to Cannes via Cabris, Spéracèdes and the Massif de Tanneron.

This excursion from Cannes to Grasse follows the N85 north of Cannes. Allow a whole day. The total mileage is about 40km (25 miles)

After his return from exile in Elba, Napoleon arrived in Cannes with a few of his trusted men. The next morning he began his arduous march through the Alps to Grenoble. We follow his course as far as Grasse.

Mougins, amid a landscape reminiscent of Tuscany, is certainly worth a visit, not only for the many excellent restaurants – the best of which is the **Moulin de Mougins**, featuring the *cuisine du soleil* of master chef Roger Vergé and located in an old oil mill – but also because this well-preserved town is among the most beautiful in the region. Its **Musée de la Photographie** (Porte Sarrasine, tel: 04 93 75 85 67; 10am–noon and 2–6pm Wed–Sat, 2–6pm Sun; July–Sep daily 10am–8pm; closed Nov and some bank holidays) is worth visiting for portraits of Picasso by photographers, including Lartigue and Brassäi.

Musician Jacques Brel used to live at **71 Rue des Lombards**; the Belgian kings Leopold and Baudoin stayed in the former **Hôtel La Pax**; Yves St Laurent spent his holidays in the **Villa Santa Lucia**, and the Moreaus and Deneuves lived in **La Grâce Dieu**. Picasso spent the last years of his life down the hill near the **Chapelle Notre Dame de la Vie**, surrounded by cypresses and olive trees.

The Scents of Grasse

Once you've driven past Mouans-Sartoux you can begin to make out **Grasse**. In times past the village was a health resort for VIPs, including the likes of Queen Victoria and Napoleon's sister, Pauline. After Catherine de Medici imported from Italy the trend of wearing perfumed gloves,

Above: the shoreline near Grasse
Left: a decisive 'nose'

the logical step was taken to begin producing the necessary scents in Grasse. In the 18th century several firms were processing mimosa, needle furze, and orange flowers, roses, lavender, jasmine and hyacinths by the ton into minute amounts of concentrate for the wealthy. Today Grasse is one of the most important perfume manufacturing cities in the world.

You can tour the large perfume factories of **Fragonard** (in the centre of town), **Galimard** and **Molinard**. The **Musée International de la Parfumerie** (8 Place du Cours, tel: 04 93 36 80 20; 10am–7pm; 10am–12.30pm and 2–5.30pm, closed Tues; closed Nov and some bank holidays) covers every aspect of the industry. It's even possible to study perfume-making at the Grasse Institute of Perfume, a private school that trains some of the best 'noses'.

A tour of the old city will take you about three hours, beginning behind the **Notre-Dame-du-Puy Cathedral**, where you can see a triptych by Bréa, a Fragonard and three oil paintings by Rubens. The old city is still primarily orientated towards the needs of the locals, which is what makes it particularly interesting for tourists. The **Place aux Aires** is especially attractive; every morning a small market is held there.

Jean Honoré Fragonard (1732–1806) was a native of Grasse who was awarded the Prix de Rome at the age of 20 and rapidly progressed to become a fashionable painter of the Paris aristocracy. However, he got into financial difficulties after the Revolution and had to return to Grasse. Later he eked out a paltry living in Paris until his death. You can see a few examples of his work in the **Villa-Musée Fragonard** (23 Boulevard Fragonard, tel: 04 93 36 01 61; June–Sep daily 10am–7pm; Oct–May, Tues–Sun, 10am–12.30pm and 2–6pm, closed some bank holidays), the glovemaker's house where he hid during the Revolution.

Back to Cannes

Take a slightly roundabout but attractive route back to Cannes, leaving Grasse by the D4 to **Cabris**, where many artists have settled. On Christmas Eve people come to take part in the nativity procession through the village. In this region, nativity figures and *santons*, models of saints, are traditionally made out of unfired clay.

Next take the D11 to **Spéracèdes**, with its mill and wash-houses, and continue on to the D562, where you should turn right towards Draguignan. Branch left on to the D94 which leads you down to the **Auberge de St-Cassien-des-Bois**. Next to the auberge there is a charming chapel dating from the 12th century. If, despite the stern signs forbidding it, you dare to set foot along the path, you will be rewarded by a lovely view of a picturesque river valley, a tributary of Lake St Cassien and a rectangular defence tower with only one window.

At the next intersection turn left on to the D38, which you should follow through the little-developed Massif de Tanneron with forests of mimosa and eucalyptus. These were replanted after a forest fire in 1970. At Mandelieu you join the heavily-travelled N7 which leads back to Cannes.

Right: portrait in the Villa-Musée Fragonard

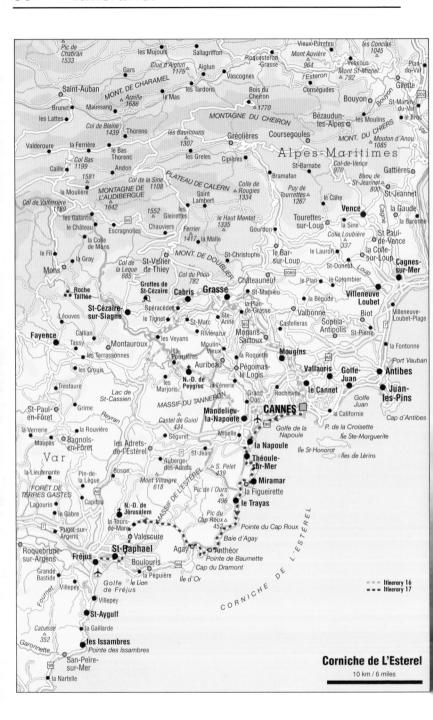

Corniche de L'Esterel

Itinerary 16
Itinerary 17

10 km / 6 miles

17. CANNES TO ST RAPHAEL *(see map, p60)*

The Esterel mountains; Théoule with its yacht harbour and beaches; Miramar; views from the coastal road; St Raphaël and the neighbouring historic town of Fréjus.

This excursion (45km/28 miles) follows the Corniche d'Or (N98) west of Cannes. Allow a whole day, especially in summer

The **Corniche d'Or**, which passes through a landscape of unique beauty, was laid out in 1903 on the initiative of the Touring Club de France. This section of coastline differs greatly from the stretch between Menton and Cannes. Here the imposing Esterel mountains, around 300 metres (1,000ft) high, with wild red cliffs of volcanic stone, have prevented development. The landscape is dominated by spruces, pines, chestnuts, eucalyptus and cork-oaks; numerous little coves tempt you to take a swim, and footpaths lead up to the summits from where you can survey the whole of this dramatic coastline.

The highest peak is **Mont Vinaigre** (618 metres/2,027ft). In the olden days mailcoaches were held up and robbed at this point. The mountain range is cut by deep gorges which extend down to the sea, where the waves break against vertical rock walls, indented capes, minute inlets and *calanques* (fjord-like bays). They also wash up against semi-submerged rocks and green islands.

Mimosa and Sculpture

As you follow the coast road out of Cannes, you come first to **La Napoule**, situated on the banks of the River Siagne at the foot of Mont San Peyré, and part of Mandelieu, which is so famous for its mimosa. The old castle in La Napoule was restored by the American sculptor Henry Clews. Displays of his work are on show inside (Avenue Henry Clews, tel: 04 93 49 95 05; guided visits Mar–Oct, closed Tues).

The next stop is **Théoule-sur-Mer**, once a busy harbour, and now popular for its sheltered beaches. It is here that Louis Féraud found the inspiration for his

Above: the imposing Esterel mountains
Right: souvenir of the port

wondrously colourful fashion collections, and he commented, 'Here is the cradle of my success, the origin of my creativity.' Eighty percent of the land belonging to the town has been declared a 'green zone', and 102km (65 miles) of hiking paths criss-cross the forested hinterland. Richelieu was attracted to the area – he had a castle built right on the sea when the Spaniards were in possession of the Lérins Islands.

Caves, Bays and Views

Above Théoule is a villa which appears to consist of bull's-eye windows stacked on top of each other. It was designed by the Hungarian-born Antti Lovag, a student of the architect Couelle, for his personal use. The holiday settlement, **Port La Galère**, located in a wooded area on a cliff above the bay of La Napoule, was created by Couelle himself, the inventor of 'habitable sculpture'. The peculiar cave-like holes in their exterior walls allow the houses to blend into the cliffs. The beach below is one of the most beautiful on the coast, although it is reserved for residents and guests of the private complex.

The exclusive seaside resort of **Miramar** has a private yacht harbour in La Figueirette Bay. The region's first fish farm was established in the bay

in 1986; it now produces 30 tons of silver bream and bass per year.

As you continue your drive round the coast towards **Anthéor**, there are two places where it is worth stopping your car to admire the view: the **Pointe de l'Observatoire** and the **Pic du Cap Roux**, both of which afford splendid panoramas over the red rocks and deep blue sea. The well-protected bay of **Agay**, which is overlooked by the 288-metres (945-ft) **Rastel d'Agay**, was a favourite spot of the Ligurians, Greeks and Romans. From here, you can take the deserted roads inland to the **Pic de l'Ours**, **Mont Vinaigre** and the **Malpey Ranger Station**, where the elegant criminal boss, Gaspard de Besse, managed his shady business in the 18th century. Also hidden in the Esterel Mountains is a lake, which is pleasant for a swim. This area teems with wild boar (normally too well fed to be dangerous).

Alternatively you can continue along the road to **Valescure**, passing on the way **Cap Esterel**. The Cap is the location of a holiday centre modelled on a Provençal village.

St Raphaël, a pretty little seaside resort (only 4½ hours from Paris on the TGV), was originally a Roman holiday centre before being plundered by the Saracen pirates. In the 10th century it belonged to the Lérins monks, and passed to the custody of the Knights Templar 200 years later. Napoleon landed here on his return from Egypt; he also departed from here 14 years later when he was banished to Elba.

Alphonse Karr, chief editor of *Le Figaro* during the 19th century, was responsible for St Raphaël becoming the fashionable resort it is today. He lived

Above: café in St Raphael
Top right: bishop's tomb in Fréjus Cathedral. **Right**: Fréjus beach

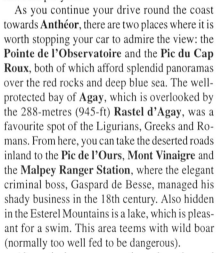

in Nice until he discovered St Raphaël and encouraged his friends to follow him down the coast. Those that did include Dumas, de Maupassant, Berlioz and Gounod. The latter composed his *Romeo and Juliet* here. Erika Mann described St Raphaël as a 'stately old-fashioned Riviera town'.

Today the city, which has a population of around 30,000, is home to the seven harbours and the **Musée Archéologique** (tel: 04 94 19 25 75; 10am–noon and 2.30–5.30pm Oct–May; 10am–noon and 3–6.30pm June–Sep; closed Sun, Mon and bank holidays), which has a collection of amphorae. In the garden stands a Roman milestone that once stood on the Via Aurelia.

Episcopal City

The neighbouring city of **Fréjus** (population 48,000) – Caesar's Forum Julii – was located on an extension of the Via Aurelia, which went through Gaul to Spain. Emperor Augustus had galleys built here. Around the time of the birth of Christ, Fréjus was the second-largest Roman harbour in the western Mediterranean. The Roman **Arena**, originally built to accommodate 10,000 spectators, was one of the oldest in Gaul. Although fairly badly damaged, it is still used today in summer for bullfights and rock concerts.

The ancient **episcopal city** (tel: 04 94 51 26 30; guided tours Tues–Sun 9am–noon and 2–5pm, daily 9am–7pm Apr–Sep; closed bank holidays) is in the centre of present-day Fréjus at the Place Formigé. The 45-minute tour includes a 4th-century baptistry, the Cathedral (open mornings and 4–6pm) dating from the 10th and 12th centuries and a 13th-century cloister; the former bishop's palace now houses the town hall. **Fréjus Plage** is a development of apartment blocks and hotels running the length of a fine flat sandy beach by the new yacht basin of Port Fréjus with mooring for 700 yachts. Plans are afoot to open up a channel originally dug by the Romans, which will lead into the centre of the town, connecting it to the sea as in Roman times.

west of cannes

18. FROM FRÉJUS TO ST TROPEZ BAY *(see map below)*

A picnic in the beautiful Massif des Maures; the holiday resort of St Aygulf, fashionable Ste Maxime; Port Grimaud.

This itinerary (35km/22 miles) takes a full day, with a morning in the Massif des Maures and an afternoon in St Tropez

Contrary to popular belief, the **Massif des Maures** was not named after the Moorish invaders, but is rather a derivation of the Greek *amauros*, which was corrupted in the Provençal dialect to *maouro*, meaning gloomy or dark. This explanation seems more poetic to me, since dark forests are an essential characteristic of the Massif: oak forests with an underbrush consisting of gorse and myrrh bushes, briars (the roots of which are made into smoking pipes), pine forests, chestnut groves and the cork-oaks whose bark is cut off every seven years to produce stoppers for bottles.

It is beautiful and lonely in these forests, whose gently rolling hills are interspersed here and there with olive trees, sheep grazing amid crimson poppies, and the occasional field filled with rows of vines. Olives, bread, sheep's cheese and a bottle of good red wine – such a picnic befits the landscape and forms an exquisite pleasure in its simplicity. The contrast between the bustling resort towns and this quiet landscape couldn't be greater. Only a short distance away from the hubbub you feel as though you're in another world.

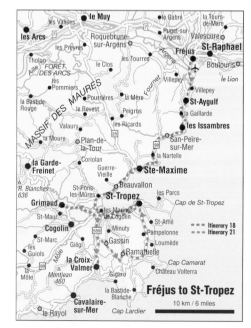

Fréjus to St-Tropez
10 km / 6 miles

When you have had your fill, return to the coast at St Aygulf for the drive to St Tropez, which you should aim to reach shortly after sunset.

St Aygulf has a beautiful, long beach – one of the Riviera's few relatively unspoilt stretches of sand. West of the town, you can climb down the cliffs to the little hidden beaches of **Les Issambres, San Pëïre, Val d'Esquières** and **La Garonnette**. These are all perfect places for a late-afternoon swim.

To Port Grimaud

The **Gulf of St Tropez** begins at the town of **Ste Maxime** – where the villas become large again, and you re-enter the land of the obviously rich and famous. This fashionable resort, situated on the north shore of the bay, has fishing and yachting harbours, as well as a sandy beach. The restored **old quarter** is reserved for pedestrians. The Lérins monks erected the rectangular tower in front of the harbour for defence purposes. Later it served as a court building and today it houses the **Musée des Arts et Traditions Locales** (Place des Aliziers, tel: 04 94 96 70 30; 10am–noon and 3–6pm, till 7pm July and Aug; closed Mon am and Tues). The **church** has an altar made of green marble from the Chartreuse de La Verne (*see page 66*).

Guy de Maupassant's family once lived in **Villa Béthanie** in Ste Maxime, not far from the casino, to the left past the Traverse Granier. This active little town now has three nightclubs, a casino and many different festivals and events (folklore, concerts, fireworks and exhibitions), not to mention the usual Riviera choice of restaurants.

Ten km (6 miles) inland on the D25 towards Le Muy, the **Musée du Phonograph et de la Musique Mécanique** (Parc St Donat, tel: 04 94 96 50 52; 10am–noon and 3–6pm; closed Mon and Tues and October to Easter) has an interesting collection of over 300 musical automatons.

Port Grimaud is situated at the far end of the bay. It was designed during the 1950s and 1960s by architect François Spoerry, who obtained a piece of marshland at the mouth of the River Giscle in 1962 and then had to wait four years to get planning permission to build. The inspiration is typically Provençal, but each house has a waterfront and a boat mooring. In theory cars are not allowed inside the village, and transport is provided by boats. Some 2,500 colourfully painted houses line the streets; shady, flower-filled squares invite one to linger a while, and small bridges span the canals.

The complex is one of France's top tourist attractions and although sometimes regarded as childishly contrived, it is a successful example of contemporary architecture – so much so, in fact, that a second similar village, **Port Cogolin**, has been constructed just along the coast.

Located just 5km (3 miles) inland, the beautifully kept medieval village of **Grimaud** is located below the ruins of its fortress. The serpentine portals and basalt arcades in the Rue du Templier are impressive. A simple Provençal meal can be enjoyed at the **Café de France** on the village square.

Left: refreshing watermelons
Right: Port Grimaud

19. LA GARDE FREINET *(see map, p64)*

A picturesque Provençal village in the Massif des Maures; a hikers' paradise; dinner on the terrace of La Faucado

From Port Grimaud it is about 20km (12 miles) inland to La Garde Freinet. Chartreuse de la Verne is a further 30km (20 miles)

La Garde Freinet, formerly named Fraxinet, is situated in the heart of the Massif des Maures in a beautiful natural forest area. The village, located at an altitude of about 400 metres (1,300ft) between the fertile Argens Plain and the Gulf of St Tropez, was occupied in the 9th century by the Saracens, who stayed for over a century. They taught the people of Provence how to use cork-oak and produce pine tar, and they introduced ceramic tiles and the tambourine to the area.

The Saracens built a fortress on the hill above the village which served as the starting point for their coastal raids. Count William of Arles finally managed to drive them out permanently in 973AD. The village is worthy of exploration, with its many fountains and little alleyways as well as its Renaissance church and old wash-house. Along the way you'll find shops selling jams made of local chestnuts as well as the candied fruits *(marrons glacés)*.

Recommended Hikes

The area is a hikers' paradise, and walks of varying lengths are detailed in a brochures available at the tourist office in La Garde Freinet. The walk up to the fortress ruins takes about half an hour, after which you are rewarded with a splendid view. It takes about 20 minutes to get to the so-called **Roches Blanches** – the White Rocks. Further hiking excursions can be made to the hamlets of La Mourre, Valdegilly, Nid du Duc, Bas-Olivier, Camp de la Suyère, Val d'Aubert and Gagnal. The terrace of **La Faucado**

(see page 78) is one of the nicest places to have lunch in La Garde Frenet.

The **Chartreuse de la Verne** (tel: 04 94 48 08 00; 11am–5pm, till 6pm Apr–Oct; closed Tues, Jan and religious holidays; silence obligatory for visitors) is located only around 30km (20 miles) away from La Garde Freinet. Heading back towards Grimaud, turn right onto the D48 and after a kilometre or so (approx. 2 miles), turn right again onto the D14, a beautiful road, running through chestnut groves and cork-oak forests. Then turn off to the left for the rough road that leads to the Charterhouse. Founded in 1170, this beautiful, semi-ruined sanctuary was abandoned by revolution-fearing monks in 1792, and is now occupied by nuns from the order of Bethlehem.

Left: Chartreuse de la Verne

20. ST TROPEZ *(see map below)*

View from the Citadel; a game of boules on the Place des Lices; a drink on the waterfront.

St Tropez is a round-the-clock place, and can be explored any time

If you believe the legend, this port city – on the southern shore of one of the most beautiful bays on the Côte d'Azur – owes its name to a Roman soldier by the name of Tropez, who was converted to Christianity during the reign of Nero. This cost him his head. His decapitated corpse was placed in a boat with a dog and a rooster (which were supposed to devour it) and abandoned to the waves. However, miraculously, it landed undamaged on the beach of present-day St Tropez.

In memory of the martyr, the *Bravade* takes place every year on 16 May – a spectacular and very loud procession in which a gilded wooden bust of the saint is carried through the city. A second *Bravade*, on 15 June, commemorates the year 1637, when the people of St Tropez fended off an attack by 22 Spanish galleons which were attempting to plunder the town and capture the four royal ships anchored in the harbour. At the end of the 19th century, Guy de Maupassant wrote of this sleepy fishing village: 'What an enchanting and simple daughter of the sea! You can smell the fish-catch, the burning tar, the brine. The scales of sardines glitter on the cobblestones like pearls.' Quite a lot has changed since then, but the same sense of enchantment remains.

Paul Signac, who came here to paint, was so taken with the town that he decided to stay. He bought

Above: St Tropez

the estate called La Hune and invited many painters to come and visit: Matisse, Marquet, Bonnard, Picabia, Van Dongen, Utrillo and Dufy, to name but a few. Their works are exhibited in the **Musée de l'Annonciade** (Place Georges Grammont, tel: 04 94 97 04 01; 10am–noon and 2–6pm or 3–7pm Jun–Sept; closed Tues, Nov and some bank holidays).

In 1925, the author Colette settled on the peninsula. She used to swim nude in the sea in front of her villa, La Treille Muscate. Not long after, the first nightclubs for rich tourists were established and the village grew fashionable. Actor Errol Flynn and author and diarist Anaïs Nin – one of Henry Miller's muses – were regular visitors. After World War II, Jean Cocteau and the Paris literati discovered St Tropez, as did the unforgettable Juliette Greco.

The town's fortune was sealed in 1959, when director Roger Vadim shot *And God Created Woman* starring Brigitte Bardot. BB bought La Madrague estate, only 300 metres (1,000ft) from Colette's former residence, which she still visits from time to time. In July and August up to 80,000 people visit St Tropez every day, whereas there are only 5,500 permanent residents.) Juliette Greco still lives here, but the town's most illustrious residents are nowadays more likely to hail from business and politics than from the world of show business.

Exploring St Tropez

It is easy to understand the attraction. St Tropez has a unique charm that it manages to retain even in the overcrowded summer months. It is the only town on the Riviera facing northwards, which gives a special quality to the evening sunlight as it reflects off the dull-pink and ochre walls. This is one reason why so many painters came here, and why so many other visitors have been inspired to paint for the first time.

If you climb up the hill to the **Citadel** at sunset and take in the view of the bay, the harbour and the town with its narrow alleyways and the grey-green tower of the church, then you will recognise the 'colourful shadows' which so fascinated Bonnard. Wander through the old streets and you will see that

behind the scenes life goes on much as it always has in this once sleepy fishing village: at the authentic fish market near the quay (the town still has around eight fishing boats which make daily deliveries to the restaurants and the daily fish market), in the cafés with their worn-out table-tops, in the arcaded **Rue de la Miséricorde**, the **Rue Allard** and on the **Place des Lices**.

Fish used to be cleaned in the shade of the plane trees on the Place des Lices; now a market is held there on Tuesdays and Saturday mornings and the locals play *boules* with the *coco parisien du showbiz*, as they refer to Parisian show-business people. To keep posted on the gossip, locals hang out in the **Café des Arts**; as tourists you would do better to listen to Radio St-Tropez (91.5FM).

St Tropez would not be what it is today without **Sénéquier**, **Le Gorille** and the **Café de Paris** – the trendy places overlooking the harbour. In the early evening Sénéquier's terrace is the ideal spot from which to watch the yacht owners sipping their cocktails on the aft-deck. At peak times in summer St Tropez is pretty well cut-off from the rest of Provence by interminable traffic jams, but just a few steps from the centre of town there is a mini-airport, with a helicopter service to Nice Airport. The most beautiful place to stay in St Tropez is without doubt the lovely **Hôtel La Ponche**, in the old fishing quarter.

21. WHERE THE CRICKETS CHIRP *(see pull-out)*
La Croix Valmer; Cap Lardier; Gassin; Ramatuelle.

This 40-km (25-mile) round-trip from St Tropez takes about three hours

Departing from St Tropez, take the D98a to La Foux and then turn left onto the D559. The village of **La Croix Valmer** is a popular health resort, whose stately villas and vineyards are protected from cold winds by oak, pine and eucalyptus-covered hills. The attractive Bouillabaisse Beach is overcrowded in the summer; the path along the coast to Cap Lardier yields quieter spots and is a pleasant walk.

Gassin is a typical Provençal village, 200 metres (650ft) above the Gulf of St Tropez. Affording wonderful views a little further on are **Les Moulins de Paillas**, which opperated as mills until the start of the 20th century. **Ramatuelle**, a well-kept secret among those who find St Tropez too crowded, has been shaped by three episodes in its history: the occupation by the Saracens in AD892, almost total destruction in 1592 because of religious conflicts between Catholics and the Protestant Henry IV, and World War II. The **Festival Gérard Philippe** has been held here every August since 1984 (Philippe's grave is in the Ramatuelle cemetery).

Leave Ramatuelle by the D61, then turn left onto the D93. The **Chapelle St Anne** is set in the shade of huge trees on a volcanic cone. The little road, into which we make a right turn to reach the chapel, leads back to St Tropez.

Top left: St Tropez's hilltop Citadel. **Left**: end of the pier show
Right: Ramatuelle

Leisure
Activities

SHOPPING

If you like shopping you'll like the French Riviera. Whether your preference is for flea markets or designer stores, it's all here. Every town has its weekly or daily market which offers a cornucopia of produce. Look out for locally made pottery and fabrics, especially the traditional *Indiennes* patterns of Provence, made into a wide varierty of items like shirts, skirts, table-cloths and napkins.

Nice, Cannes and Antibes all have famous daily markets, as well as antiques and flower markets *(see page 73)*. Antiques are never cheap, but you can always find interesting small items which are easy to transport home, such as glass, lace and linen, at reasonable prices.

Local produce makes very good gifts; look out for lavender products – perfumes, oils and lavender bags – exquisitely packaged soaps, jars of honey, nuts, olive oil, jars of locally made *tapenade* (olive paste) and candied fruit, violets and rose petals. Bunches or packets of locally dried herbs also make easy, lightweight gifts to take home, as do *tisanes* – dried flowers, camomile, verveine, or lime-flower, which make wonderful teas and can be bought loose from the market or in packets from the pharmacy. In season you can also buy dried local mushrooms, such as morels or ceps.

The bigger towns have large shopping malls, and streets lined with the latest designer stores; for expensive fashions, head for Cannes or Monaco. Large department stores in town centres include Monoprix, Prisunic, and Galeries Lafayette. Everywhere you will find large supermarkets (Casino, Auchan and Carrefour), which in addition to regular groceries can yield good take-home buys, such as cheap espadrilles or well-designed tableware.

Left: marionnette shop in Tourettes-sur-Loup. **Right**: market wares

Nice and Around

The Avenue Jean Médecin is Nice's main shopping street; it includes the Galeries Lafayette department store and Nice Etoile. Luxury boutiques are also found in the pedestrian zone in the Rue Masséna/ Rue de France.

A flea market is held on Monday on the Cours Saleya between the old quarter and the sea. At the other end of the scale,the imposing shopping centre Cap 3000 is located just behind the airport. This has countless boutiques to suit every budget. Early-bird shoppers already thinking of Christmas should look out for nativity figures and statues of saints made of unfired clay, called *santons* – these are very popular in Provence.

In **La Colle sur Loup** there is a street full of antique shops; in summer (Jun–mid-Sep), the boutiques of **Juan-les-Pins** are open until 11pm and later. You can buy beautiful glasses in **Biot** in the Verrerie de Biot. Those who like lithography might like to look in at the Fondation Maeght in **St Paul-de-Vence**.

Cannes and Around

The **Rue d'Antibes** – parallel to the Croisette – is the main shopping street of Cannes. It is often compared with the Rue de Faubourg St-Honoré, and the prices are as inflated here as they are there. Each Saturday there is a flea market with relatively reasonable prices in the **Allées de la Liberté** across from the Palais des Festivals. The **Rue Meynadier** is well known for its gourmet food stores.

You can buy *eau de toilette* and good soap in perfume capital **Grasse**, while Picasso made **Vallauris** famous as a pottery centre; here, you can buy beautiful majolica in the Galerie Madoura.

SPECIALITY SHOPS

Olives and Olive Products

Alziari Boutique: 14 Rue St François de Paule, Nice. Tel: 04 93 85 76 92.
Nice @rt: 14 Rue Hôtel des Postes, Nice. Tel: 04 93 85 65 52.
Maison de l'Olive: 18 Rue Pairolière, Nice. Tel: 04 93 80 01 61.
Moulin a Huile: 138 Route de Draguignan, Grasse. Tel: 04 93 70 21 42.

Candied Fruits and Flowers

Confiserie Florian: 14 Quai Papacino, Nice. Tel: 04 93 55 43 50. (Also: Confiserie Florian: Pont du Loup. Tel: 04 93 59 33 20.) Both shops make and sell the same products – including candied rose petals – and give free guided visits of the workshops and free tastings.

Flowers

Massa Horticulture: 597 Chemin de Crémat, Nice. Tel: 04 93 37 80 02.

Santons

La Couqueto: 8 Rue St François de Paule, Nice. Tel 04 93 80 90 30.
Le Maïoun: 1 Rue du Marché, Nice. Tel: 04 93 13 05 75.

Clothes and Fabrics

Les Olivades: 8 Avenue de Verdun, Nice. Tel: 04 93 88 75 50. Local fabrics – the last of this kind still printed in Provence.
Rondini: 16 Rue Clemenceau, St Tropez. Tel: 04 94 97 19 55. Classic Tropezienne leather sandals.

Pottery

Roger Collet: Montée Ste-Anne, Vallauris. Tel: 04 93 64 65 84.
Plat Jérôme: 34 Rue Centrale, Nice. Tel: 04 93 62 17 09.

Wine

Château de Bellet: St Roman de Bellet, Nice. Tel: 04 93 37 81 57.
Château de Crémat: 442 Chemin de Crémat, Nice. Tel: 04 92 15 12 15.

Perfume

Parfumerie Molinard: 60 Boulevard Victor Hugo, Grasse. Tel: 04 93 36 01 62.
Parfumerie Galimard: 73 Route de Cannes, Grasse. Tel: 04 93 09 20 00.
Le Studio des Fragrances: Les 4 Chemins, Grasse. Factory prices.

shopping

Parfumerie Fragonard: 20 Boulevard Fragonard, Grasse. Tel: 04 93 36 44 65. http://www.fragonard.com

Glassware
Verrerie de Biot: Chemin des Combes, Biot. Tel: 04 93 65 03 00.

MARKETS

These are extremely popular in France. Every small town will have at least one street market.

Antibes
General market
Cours Masséna: daily except Monday, from 6am–1pm.
Flea market
Place Audiberti: Saturday.
Handicrafts
Cours Masséna: Tuesday, Thursday, Friday and Sunday, starting at 3pm.
Clothing
Place du Tribunal: Tuesday and Saturday.

Cagnes-sur-Mer
General market
Town centre: daily except Monday.

Cannes
General market
Forville Market and Rue Maynadier: daily except Monday.
Flower market
Rue Félix Faure: daily except Monday.
Flea market.
Rue Félix Faure: Saturday.

Fréjus
General market
Town centre: Wednesday and Saturday mornings.
Flower market
Place Formigé: Wednesday and Saturday mornings.

Grasse
General market
Cours Honoré Cresp: Wednesday.

Menton
General market
Halles: every morning; 'large market' on Saturday mornings.
Flea market
Esplanade Francis Palmero: second Sunday of the month.

Monaco
General market
Condamine Market/Monte Carlo Market: every morning.

Nice
Produce and flowers
Saleya Market/Liberation Market/Fontaine du Temple Market: every morning except Monday.
Flea market
Cours Saleya: Monday.
Fish market
Place St François: every morning except Monday.

St Tropez
General market
Place des Lices: Tuesday and Saturday morning.

Vence
General market
Place Clémenceau: 'little market' every Tuesday morning and a 'large market' on Friday mornings.

Left: bric-a-brac
Above: images of St Tropez

EATING OUT

Jacques Médécin, the legendary mayor of Nice – and the region's most powerful man before his disgrace for cronyism and financial misdemeanours in the 1980s and death in 1998 – was also the author of a cookery book entitled *Cuisine Niçoise*, which goes to show what an important role the kitchen plays in French society. I can't judge the extent of Médécin's crimes, but his cook book certainly holds its own in this country of gourmets.

Fortunately, after a recent, but thankfully brief, flirtation with *nouvelle cuisine*, the master chefs of the Riviera, of whom there are quite a few, have returned to traditional regional recipes – though often incorporating new ideas and healthier choices than in pre-*nouvelle cuisine* days. In order to help you decipher the menus, and make the most of the local dishes, several of the best specialities are listed below.

Pissaladière is a delicious onion pie, flavoured with anchovy purée (*pissala*) and local black olives. *Socca* is a type of thin pancake made of chick pea flour. For *ratatouille* each of the vegetables (typically tomatoes, aubergines, red and green peppers, and courgettes) are cooked separately and not mixed together until immediately before serving. *Tourte de bléa* is a pie which is filled with beet greens, currants and almonds or pine nuts.

Salade niçoise, if properly prepared, must consist of salad greens, cucumber slices, tomatoes, black olives, hard-boiled eggs, onions, tuna fish and anchovy fillets, all mixed together with just a little olive oil. Optional extra ingredients might include small artichokes or green peppers.

Mesclun is a hearty-tasting salad which always includes dandelion and hedge-mustard leaves. *Petits farcis* are artichoke hearts, baby courgettes or tomatoes stuffed with a spicy minced-meat filling and served *gratiné*. The delicious *beignets des courgettes* are courgette flowers dipped in batter and then deep fried – a true delicacy, and one of the world's rare flavours. *Tripe à la niçoise* is prepared with tomatoes, carrots and lots of garlic. It is the one tripe dish that even dedicated adversaries should taste. *Stocaficada* is a stew of dried codfish.

Everything which has *pistou* in its name contains basil, the ubiquitious herb of the Mediterranean summer. For example, a vegetable soup is transformed when a paste of basil, garlic and olive oil is added. This is equally true of pâtés and pasta. The latter is mixed with *pistou* and topped off with a lavish sprinkling of Parmesan cheese. *Gnocchi, ravioli* and pizza taste just as good here as they do in Italy.

Daube is large cubes of beef cooked until tender over a low flame in red wine with cinnamon and lemon peel. *Pan bagnat* –

Above: fresh grilled fish

white bread soaked with olive oil and layered with greens, onions, tomatoes, hard-boiled eggs and tuna fish – is sold on the beaches as well as served in restaurants, and is a refreshing delicacy in the heat of the mid-afternoon. *Violets* are the small young artichokes without which no crudité basket is worth its name; they are eaten raw. *Aïoli* is a garlic-flavoured mayonnaise; it is served on Fridays with boiled fish and vegetables, a gesture to the region's Catholic past when everyone ate fish on Friday.

Soup de poisson comes with croutons, garlic cloves, *rouille* (mayonnaise with garlic and pimentos) and a small bowl of grated cheese, which are combined according to a strict ritual: rub the croutons with the garlic cloves, lay them in the dish, place a spoonful of the delicious *rouille* on top, sprinkle cheese over it and finally pour the soup on top of the lot. A really well-prepared *bouillabaisse*, a medley of fish and flavourings, is a true speciality and is only found in a few restaurants. Because it involves numerous fresh ingredients it is not cheap, or easy to make – but it's a pleasure you shouldn't deny yourself.

The tastiest Mediterranean fish are seabass (*loup*), John Dory (*St-Pierre*), silver bream and red mullet (*rouget*); the latter should only be ordered filleted, since it has an unbelievable number of bones. Mussels and shellfish should only be eaten from September to April unless you know the restaurant very well.

The lamb in this area is also excellent. The sheep graze on grass and the fragrant herbs of Provence, endowing the meat with superb flavour.

Wine

Provence is known for its rosé wines, which form the greater part of the region's production, and which are so delicious drunk chilled in the heat of the Mediterranean sun. Côtes de Provence wines were admitted to AOC (Appellation d'Origine Contrôlée status) in 1977. Other AOC wines in the area include Cassis and Bandol, which are situated between Toulon and Marseille;

Palette, produced just outside Aix-en-Provence; and Bellet, which is produced on the hills rising directly behind Nice.

AOC is a controlled designation of origin which, within a certain region, regulates the type of grapes, the maximum output, the minimum alcohol content and the number of vines per given area. On the label, the name of the region is printed in large letters along with the words Appellation Contrôlée. VDQS means Vin Délimité de Qualité Supérieure and denotes wines of better quality from certain precisely defined areas. These rank just behind the AOC wines under French law.

Recommended wines to drink with fish and shellfish dishes are Cassis, an excellent dry white (which some claim is the only wine to serve with *bouillabaisse*), Bellet, which is dry yet fruity, or Palette. There are a great many red wines to choose from: those from Bandol and the north side of the Massif des Maures are rounded and hearty, while the more elegant and finer red wines are produced around St Tropez and the Argens Valley.

Domaine means that the wine comes from vineyards which may extend over a very large area. *Château* means a castle or estate winery. If the label indicates that the wine was bottled on the domaine or at the castle, you can be reasonably certain it is a good wine. *Vin de pays* is a simple wine of the region and may be served by the carafe.

Wines from the following vineyards, many of which can be visited for tours and wine-tastings, are found throughout the region:

Bellet
Château de Crémat, St Roman de Bellet
Bandol
Domaine Ott, La Londe les Maures
Château Vannières, La Cadière d'Azur
Château Pibarnon, La Cadière d'Azur

Right: buy your baguettes here

Cassis
Clos Ste Magdaleine

Côtes de Provence
Château Minuty, Gassin
Domaine d'Astros, near Vidauban
Domaine de la Bastide Blanche, Ramatuelle

Palette
Château Simone Palette, Meyreuil

Coteaux d'Aix
Château du Seuil, Aix-en-Provence
Comanderie de la Bargemone, RN7, St Cannat
Château Vignelaure, Route de Jonques, Rians

Beer

The French for beer is *bière*; *bière blonde* is light beer or lager-type beer; *bière brune* is dark beer, although it doesn't really equate to the British 'bitter'; *bière à la pression* is draught beer; *un bock* is a small glass of beer and *panaché* is a shandy (beer with lemonade).

Coffee and Tea

Several kinds of coffee are available; which one you order is likely to depend on the time of day as well as individual preference: *café noir* is black coffee served in small cups at any times of the day, especially after a meal; *café crème* is coffee topped up with steamed milk and served in medium-sized cups, again drunk at any time of the day; *café au lait* is a large cup of coffee with a lot of steamed milk, usually drunk by locals at breakfast time and rarely ordered later in the day (though there is no reason why you shouldn't); *un décafféiné (or simply, un déca)* is, as the name suggests, decaffeinated coffee.

As for tea, *thé au citron* is tea with lemon; *thé au lait* is tea with milk; *tisane* is herbal tea; *infusion de camomille* is camomile tea; *infusion de menthe* is peppermint tea.

RESTAURANTS

Visiting restaurants on the Côte is a genuine pleasure whether they are gourmet temples or simple bistros. The well-known food guides such as Michelin give detailed information on the huge number of options. However, personal recommendations are just as welcome (if not more so) to the food lover, and the following list is a compilation of my own favourite restaurants.

It is essential to make reservations, especially during high season. The price guide below is based on the average *prix fixe menu* per person excluding wine, the best indication of general price. It is nearly always best value to choose the *prix fixe menu*; the lunchtime version is usually cheaper than indicated here.
Expensive: menus over 40 euros
Moderate: menus 25–40 euros
Inexpensive: menus under 25 euros

I have noted where credit cards are not accepted (rarely the case). Most of the major cards are acceptable, with the occasional exception of American Express.

Antibes/Juan-les-Pins
Restaurant du Bacon
Boulevard de Bacon, Antibes
Tel: 04 93 61 50 02
This celebrated Antibes restaurant is well known for its high quality fish dishes, in particular its spectacular *bouillabaisse*. Closed Monday, Tuesday lunch and 1 November–31 January. Expensive.

Auberge Provençale
16 Place Nationale, Antibes
Tel: 04 93 34 13 24
A good value traditional bistro specialising in grills and fresh fish and seafood. Moderate.

Tétou
à La Plage, Golfe-Juan
Tel: 04 93 63 71 16
Right on the beach and considered the place to go for *bouillabaisse*, the celebrated Mediterranean fish soup. Closed Wednesday and November–February. No credit cards. Expensive.

Biot
Auberge du Jarrier
30 Passage de la Bourgade
Tel: 04 93 65 11 68
Elegant French cuisine with a Mediter-

ranean flavour. September to June closed Monday and Tuesday; July and August closed Tuesday. Moderate.

Cagnes
Entre Cour et Jardin
102 Montée de la Bourgade
Tel: 04 93 20 72 27
This lovely restaurant, tucked away in a side street, has a friendly atmosphere and stages art exhibitions twice a year in its courtyard. Closed Tuesday and lunchtime Monday to Friday. Moderate.

JosyJo
4 Place Planastel,
Haut-de-Cagnes
Tel: 04 93 20 68 76
Popular local restaurant in the medieval village, specialising in meat cooked on a charcoal fire. Closed Saturday lunchtime and Sunday, also mid-November to mid-December. Expensive.

Cannes
La Palme díOr
Hôtel Martinez
73 La Croisette
Tel: 04 92 98 74 14
Imaginative gastronomic cuisine with a taste of the Mediterranean. One of Cannes' top restaurants, with a view of the Bay and the Lérins Islands. Closed Monday and Tuesday and one month in November/December. Expensive.

Royal Gray
Hôtel Gray d'Albion, 38 Rue Serbes
Tel: 04 92 99 79 60
Now presided over by master chef Alain Roy and serving top-quality Provençal cuisine, this is still one of the finest restaurants in Cannes. Closed Sunday and Monday. Moderate-expensive.

Astoux et Brun
27 Rue Félix Faure
Tel: 04 93 39 21 87
Well located for the flower and flea market. Recommended for seafood. Moderate.

Left: wine-making in Provence
Above: *plat du jour*

La Mère Besson
13 Rue des Frères Pradignac
Tel: 04 93 39 59 24
A local favourite, this is a reasonably priced bistro serving good regional specialities and *aïoli* on Fridays. Closed lunchtime and all day Sunday. Moderate.

Charlot 1er
87 Boulevard de la Plage
Tel: 04 93 31 00 07
Popular restaurant near the sea and specialising in fish dishes. Booking is essential during high season. Closed Tuesday. Moderate.

Eze
La Chèvre d'Or
Rue du Barri
Tel: 04 92 10 66 66
Fabulous gourmet restaurant situated on the heights of Eze. Booking required. Closed mid-November to mid-March. Expensive.

Grimaud
Café de France
5 Place Neuve
Tel: 04 94 43 20 05
Simple Provençal food served on a lovely shady terrace in the village square. Closed mid-November to February. Inexpensive.

Menton
Le Lion d'Or
7 Rue des Marins
Tel: 04 93 35 74 67
Good-value local favourite serving fresh fish straight out of the sea. Closed Sunday evening and Monday September to June. Moderate.

Monaco
Café de Paris
Place du Casino, Monte Carlo
Tel: 377-92 16 20 20
This wonderfully renovated brasserie in the Belle Epoque style is one of the sights of Monte Carlo. What's more, you can dine in the Café de Paris without breaking the bank. Moderate.

Louis XV
Hôtel de Paris, Place du Casino, Monte Carlo
Tel: 377-92 16 30 01
One of the world's great restaurants, presided over by Alain Ducasse – a must for lunch if you can afford it. Vegetables served with truffles are a particular speciality. Expensive (very). **The Grill**, in the same building, is slightly more affordable and almost as glamorous.

Polpetta
2 Rue Paradis, Monte Carlo
Tel: 377-93 50 67 84
Reasonably priced restaurant in the centre of Monte Carlo, serving Italian specialities. Closed Tuesday, also two weeks in October and three weeks in June. Inexpensive.

Rampoldi
3 Avenue des Spélugues
Tel: 377 93 30 70 65
Serves classic French cuisine, good grills and Italian specialities. A great favourite with locals. Expensive.

La Garde-Freinet
La Faucado
Tel: 04 94 43 60 41
La Faucado is a countryside *auberge* with a pretty terrace (*see itinerary 19, page 66*) and serving high quality, rustic dishes such as beef with morel mushrooms. Makes a delightful lunch stop. Closed Tuesday and January to March. Moderate to expensive.

Mougins
Le Moulin de Mougins
Avenue Notre Dame de Vie
Tel: 04 93 75 78 24
Roger Vergé is the chef most responsible for promoting the fashion for Provençal cuisine, what he calls 'Cuisine du Soleil' (cuisine of the sun). Here in his original restaurant, in an ancient olive mill, you can sample classics enhanced with imaginative panache –

courgette flowers stuffed with truffles, for example, or *beignets* of flower blossoms. Closed Monday and mid-November to mid-January. Expensive.

Nice
La Mérenda
4 Rue de la Terrasse

This little bistro tucked away in Nice's old town has a big reputation. Cognoscenti drop in to make their reservations, since there's no phone. Le Merenda is celebrated for its classic Niçoise cuisine; try specialities such as stockfish, stuffed courgette flowers and beef *daube*. No credit cards. Moderate.

Les Dents de la Mer
2 Rue St-Francois de Paule
Tel: 04 93 80 99 16

Restaurant sporting a nautical theme in the old town. Specialises in fish and Niçoise dishes. Moderate.

Café de Turin
5 Place Garibaldi
Tel: 04 93 62 29 52

This is a large and bustling brasserie and café. If you like, you can get the measure of the place simply by having a morning coffee. At other times, try its excellent shellfish, especially the oysters. Closed June. Inexpensive.

Au Soleil
7 bis Rue d'Italie
Tel: 04 93 88 77 74

Good value traditional brasserie with very reasonably priced lunchtime menus. Closed Saturday, and throughout December and January. Inexpensive.

Le Safari
1 Cours Saleya
Tel: 04 93 80 18 44

Large popular café with outside tables, right by the market. Try the *bagna cauda*, anchovy dip with vegetables, or the calamari (squid) *daube*. Moderate.

Aphrodite
10 Boulevard Dubouchage
Tel: 04 93 85 63 53

A fashionable restaurant in the new town, Aphrodite is particularly known for its inventive cuisine and desserts. Closed Sunday and Monday. Moderate–inexpensive.

Chantecler
Hôtel Negresco
37 Promenade des Anglais
Tel: 04 93 16 64 00

This is Nice's grandest restaurant, serving elegantly prepared and imaginative interpretations of Mediterranean cuisine in a luxurious setting. Closed 15 November–15 December. Expensive.

Above: lunching out

L'Esquinade
5 Quai des Deux Emmanuel
Tel: 04 93 89 59 36
A well-established gourmet restaurant with an attractive position overlooking the old harbour. Recommended for fish and seafood. Closed Saturday lunchtime and Sunday. Expensive.

Peillon
Auberge de la Madone
Tel: 04 93 79 91 17
Great Provençal inn serving authentic local dishes and intriguing variations such as crab with almonds. There are fabulous views from the terrace in this mountain village only a few miles outside Nice. Closed Wednesday and 20 October to 20 December and 7–21 January. Moderate/expensive.

St Jean-Cap-Ferrat
Voile d'Or
Tel: 04 93 01 13 13
First-rate cuisine combines here with an idyllic setting overlooking the pretty harbour. Closed November to March. Expensive.

St Jeannet
Auberge St Barbe
Place St Barbe
Tel: 04 93 24 94 38
Italian-influenced cooking is offered in this rustic *auberge*; try the stuffed sardines and Niçoise-style vegetables. Inexpensive.

St Laurent-du-Var
Sant 'Ana
Port St Laurent
Tel: 04 93 07 02 24
Pleasant restaurant located on the harbour of St Laurent, recommended for seafood. Closed Monday, two weeks in November and two weeks in January. Moderate.

La Couleur Pourpre
7 Rempart Ouest
Tel: 04 93 32 60 14
Well situated in the old town, this popular restaurant serves nicely presented local cuisine and has intimate dining rooms on four levels. Closed lunchtimes July and August; rest of the year closed Wednesday and lunchtime on Thursday. Moderate.

St Paul-de-Vence
Colombe d'Or
Place Général de Gaulle
Tel: 04 93 32 80 02
This has long been known as an exquisite small hotel and gorgeous restaurant, full of stunning artworks donated by Picasso, Braque, Miró and many others when they came to what was then a village café in the 1920s. The terrace is the place to eat, and the serving of 15 different hors d'oeuvres makes for great surprises. Closed 2 November–20 December. Expensive.

St Tropez
L'Echalotte
35 Rue Général Allard
Tel: 04 94 54 83 26
L'Echalotte offers excellent value for the centre of St Tropez; eat inside or in the garden. House specialites include beef with shallots and home-made *boudin noir*. Closed Thursday October–May. Moderate.

Above: dinner in full swing

Le Petit Charron

6 Rue Charrons
Tel: 04 94 97 73 78

Local favourite, serving imaginative Mediterranean cuisine. Try the *moules marinière* with saffron, and for dessert *creme brulée* with lavender flowers. Closed lunch July to 15 September, Sunday 16 September to 30 June, 15 January to 15 February, 1 to 15 August and 15 November to 1 December. Moderate.

La Bouillabaisse

Quartier la Bouillabaisse
Tel: 04 94 97 54 00

Located in an old fisherman's cottage. You will be served excellent fish straight from the sea and can even arrive by boat. Closed Tuesday evening and Wednesdays mid-October to mid-November and mid-February to mid-May; closed mid-November to mid-February. Open daily mid-May to mid-October. Moderate.

Chez Fuch's

7 Rue des Commercants
Tel: 04 94 97 01 25

Popular bistro serving traditional French dishes. Closed Tuesday October to June. Moderate– expensive

Bistro des Lices

Place des Lices
Tel: 04 94 55 82 82

Fashionable restaurant that's great for people-watching and noted for its good quality cuisine. Moderate.

Vallauris
Gousse d'Ail

11 Avenue Grasse
Tel: 04 93 64 10 71

This is a good-value restaurant serving regional dishes with lashings of garlic. Closed Sunday evening, Monday all day, Tuesday lunch July and August; closed Sunday evening, Monday all day and Tuesday evening rest of year; also closed 1–15 July and 5–25 November. Inexpensive– moderate.

Vence
Auberge des Seigneurs

Place du Frêne
Tel: 04 93 58 04 24

Auberge serving Provençal dishes. Closed Monday, lunchtime on Tuesday to Thursday, and 15 November–15 March. Moderate.

Maximin

689 Chemin de la Gaude
Tel: 04 93 58 90 75

Chef Jacques Maximin runs this small restaurant with a tiny garden. Booking essential. Closed Sunday evening, Monday and lunchtime on Tuesday. Expensive.

Villefranche-sur-Mer
La Mère Germaine

Quai Courbet
Tel: 04 93 01 71 39

A long-time favourite – Cocteau was a regular – overlooking the fishing harbour. Serves excellent fish and seafood. Closed mid-November to Christmas. Moderate.

La Ferme St Michel

Avenue de la Condamine
Grande Corniche
Tel: 04 93 76 68 38

La Ferme St Michel is a well-located *auberge* with lovely views over the sea. It specialises in finely flavoured cutlets, steaks, kebabs and chicken grilled over a wood fire. Also known for its wide variety of delicious desserts. Closed Tuesday. Moderate.

Above: try the fish soup

NIGHTLIFE

Nightlife on the French Riviera is concentrated on the coast, and popular resorts such as Juan-les-Pins and Cannes see plenty of action. Some of the most popular nightclubs are:

Antibes/Juan les Pins
Siesta
Route du Bord de Mer
Tel: 04 93 33 31 31
An open air nightclub complete with restaurant, seven dance floors and casino. Closed November.

Pam-Pam
137 Boulevard Wilson
Tel: 04 93 61 11 05
Excellent programmed offering live Brazilian bands.

Cannes
Cat Corner
22 Rue Macé
Tel: 04 93 39 31 31
Dance till dawn.
La Chunga
24 Rue Latour-Maubourg
Tel: 04 93 94 11 29
Live music and food.

Le Zanzibar
85 Rue Félix-Faure
Tel: 04 93 39 30 75
Popular gay bar.

Monte Carlo
These clubs are concentrated in one area:
Jimmy'z:
Avenue Princesse Grace
Tel: 377-92 16 22 77
The Living Room
7 Avenue des Spélugues
Tel: 377 93 50 80 31
Monte Carlo Sporting Club
Avenue Princesse Grace
Tel: 377-92 16 22 44
From 10.45pm, mid-September to June. Disco-cum-piano bar.
Tiffany's
3 Avenue des Spélugues
Tel: 377-93 50 53 13
A perennial favourite with the over 25s. Closed Monday to Wednesday.

Nice
Chez Wayne
15 Rue de la Prefecture
Tel: 04 93 13 46 99
Rock and roll, live bands.
Le 70's
24 Quai Lunel
Tel: 04 93 55 14 42
Cool disco by the port. Closed Monday.

St Tropez
La Bodega du Papagayu
Résidence du Port
Tel: 04 94 97 76 70
Le Café de Paris
Quai Suffren
Tel: 04 94 97 00 56
Open all year round. Puts on live music in high season.
Les Caves du Roy
Avenue Paul Signac
Tel: 04 94 97 16 02
Legendary St Tropez nightclub.
The VIP Room
Résidence du Nouveau Port
Tel: 04 94 97 14 70

Above: the night is young until well past midnight

CALENDAR OF EVENTS

January
Cannes: MIDEM – international music business market.
Mandelieu: Mimosa festival.
Monaco: 26–27: Festival of Ste-Dévote (Monaco's patron saint). International Circus Festival.

February
Cannes: Mimosa festival. Antiques fair.
Menton: Lemon festival (the two weeks around Shrove Tuesday).
Nice: Carnival; begins three weeks before Shrove Tuesday (*Mardi Gras*) and ends on Ash Wednesday.
Valbonne: Grape and local produce festival.

March
Antibes/Juan-les-Pins: Antiques fair.
Fréjus: Third weekend after Easter: *Bravade* in honour of François de Paule.
Nice: Cougourdon folklore festival in Cimiez.
Roquebrune/Cap Martin: Good Friday evening Procession of the Dead Christ.
Vence: Easter Sunday and Monday: Provençal folklore with flower parade.

April
Monaco: International Tennis Tournament.

May
Cannes: International Film Festival.
Grasse: Rose Festival.
Monaco: Sunday after Ascension Day: Formula 1 Grand Prix.
St Tropez: 16–18: *Bravades*.

June
Cannes: Festival of *Café Théâtre*.
St Tropez: 15: Spanish *Bravade*.

July
Antibes/Juan-les-Pins: Jazz Festival.
Cagnes-sur-Mer: Evening trotting races at the Hippodrome.

Cap d'Antibes: Mariners' festival.
Ile Ste-Marguerite: *Son et Lumière* (until September).
Menton: 14: Bastille Day fireworks held throughout the region; musical evenings, Parc du Pian.
Monaco: Prince's Palace concerts; International Fireworks Festival.
Nice: Nice Jazz Festival; Voucalia festival of Mediterranean music.

August
Grasse: First weekend: Jasmine Festival.
Menton: Chamber music festival.
Monaco: International Fireworks Festival.
Roquebrune/Cap Martin: Procession through the old village.

September
Nice: Triathlon.
Peille: First Sunday: festival commemorating ending of a great water shortage.
St Tropez: Les Voiles de St Tropez (international sailing competition).

November
Monaco: 19 November: National Day, with parades, ceremonies and spectacles (fireworks on 18 November).

December
Fréjus: *Santon* fairs.
Lucéram: 24: traditional Shepherds' Christmas (musical blessing of lambs).

Right: festive dress in Cannes

POSTES

**HEURES
DES LEVÉES**

JOURS OUVRABLES

11H

SAMEDI

10H

BUREAU
LE PLUS PROCHE

ST. PAUL

NE PAS JETER DE JOURNAUX
DANS CETTE BOITE

Practical
Information

GETTING THERE

By Air
All major airlines from Britain and the US fly to Paris, and from Paris there are regular flights to Nice Côte d'Azur. Delta flies direct to Nice from New York.
Airport information: 08 20 42 33 33
Airport taxis (24 hrs): 04 93 13 78 78
Lost property: 04 93 21 31 11 (Terminal 1); 04 93 21 31 12 (Terminal 2)

By Rail
There is a TGV from Paris to Nice five times a day in winter, eight times a day in summer (journey time approx. 5½ hours), and also a daily TGV at least three times a day from Lille to Nice all year (journey time approx. 7½ hours).There is an autorail service from Paris (runs June to mid-December only).

The SOS Voyageurs service at Gare SNCF (Avenue Thiers, Nice. Tel: 04 93 82 62 11. Monday–Friday 9am–noon and 3–6pm) helps passengers who have lost their luggage or missed trains, and assists young mothers and the elderly.

By Coach
Gare Routière de Nice has national and international coach connections. (Promenade du Paillon. Tel:04 93 85 61 81 or 04 93 80 08 70.)

GETTING AROUND

Railway Stations (SNCF)
General Information Service
(Cannes, Nice and Marseille):
Tel: 08 36 35 35 35

Airports
Nice: Tel: 08 20 42 33 33
Marseille: Tel: 04 42 14 14 14

Left: for home thoughts
Right: follow the signs

Helicopter Services
Nice Hélicoptères: Regular flights Nice–Cannes (Palm Beach) and private hire. Tel: 04 93 21 34 32. Email: nicehelicopteres@wanadoo.fr.
Héli-Air Monaco: Scheduled services Nice–Monaco and charter flights. Tel: 377-92 05 00 50.
Héli Riviera (Cannes): Charter hire around the region. Tel: 04 93 90 40 91. Website: www.heliriviera.com

USEFUL INFORMATION

Business Hours
Large department stores and shopping centres are open weekdays 10am–noon and 3–7pm. Most food stores are closed 12.30–4pm. Shops on the market streets are open on Sunday and holidays until 12.30pm. Many are closed on Monday. Banks open Monday–Friday 8.30am–noon and 1.30–4.30pm. State museums are closed Tuesday and holidays (municipal museums close Monday); churches are frequently shut from noon–2pm. Many museums and some hotels close in November.

Electrical Equipment
The local electric current is 220 volts, with two-pin plugs.

Tipping
Gratuities are usually included in the bill in hotels, restaurants and cafés but it is usual to leave a little extra. Hairdressers, taxi drivers, porters and doormen expect a small tip.

MONEY MATTERS
Banks/Bureaux de Change
Travellers' cheques can only be cashed with a passport or other form of personal identification. Most banks have automatic cash dispensers and offer currency exchange services. (*See* also *page 85.*)

The **Change Or/Office Provençal** exchange office (17 Avenue Thiers, tel: 04 93 88 56 80) is open daily, 7.30am–9pm. Other bureaux open on Sundays include **Thomas Cook** in the Nice railway station; the **Bureau de Change** in Nice Airport; and **Cofima**, 2 Rue de France, Nice.

Credit Cards
American Express, Visa (Carte Bleu), Diners Club and Eurocard Mastercard are the most frequently honoured. You can't use cards in markets or in some of the smaller hotels and restaurants.

COMMUNICATION & MEDIA
Telephone
Most public telephones require a telephone card available at post offices and tobacco shops.

To dial other countries (including Monaco from France), dial the international access code 00 then the country code: Australia (61); Ireland (353); UK (44); US and Canada (1). If using a US credit phone card, dial the company's access number: Sprint, tel: 0800-99-0087; AT&T, tel: 0800-99-0011; MCI, tel: 0800-99-0019.

Post Offices (PTT)
The *Bureaux de Poste* are open Monday–Friday 9am–6pm (some 9am–noon and 2–6pm) and Saturday 9am–noon.

Newspapers and Magazines
Nice Matin is the regional daily paper. You can also buy the *International Herald Tribune* on the morning of publication, as you can the London *Guardian,* printed in Marseille; other foreign-language newspapers are generally available by the afternoon. *La Semaine et des Spectacles* and *L'Officiel des Loisirs* are weekly guides to local events. English-language publications include the *Riviera Reporter* newspaper, produced every two months.

Radio and Television
Riviera Radio (106.3 FM in Monaco; 106.5FM in France) is an English-language station broadcasting from Monte Carlo. It buys BBC World Service programmes. Radio France Internationale broadcasts news in English (89 FM).

Many of the larger hotels have Sky News and CNN. Some foreign films are shown in their original language on French TV and on Télévision Monte-Carlo.

Above: a great way to get around

PUBLIC HOLIDAYS

1 January	New Year's Day
Easter Monday	No fixed date
1 May	Labour Day
8 May	Armistice Day (1945)
Ascension	No fixed date
Pentecost	No fixed date
14 July	Bastille Day
15 August	Assumption
1 November	All Saints' Day
11 November	Armistice Day (1918)
25 December	Christmas Day

EMERGENCIES

Police: Tel: 17
Fire Department: Tel: 18
Ambulance: Tel: 15

Lost Credit Cards
Visa: Tel: 0800-90 11 79
MasterCard: Tel: 0800-90 13 87
American Express: Tel: 0800-90 86 00

ON THE ROAD

Driving
The use of safety belts is mandatory in France. Similarly motorcycle riders must wear helmets and keep their lights on day and night.

Speed Limits: in town the limit is 50kmh (31 mph), while on normal roads it will be 90kmh (56 mph) and on motorways (*autoroutes*) 130kmh (80 mph). The motorways are generally toll roads; if you have coins and do not require change, when you get to the toll booths follow the signs reading *automatique*.

In the case of accidents which damage only property, try to avoid a shouting match and fill out the *constat à l'amiable* insurance form.

Note that petrol is expensive in France.

Maps
Detailed, large-scale maps, useful for walking and cycling, are published by the Institut Géographique Nationale (IGN). The best scale series is 10cm to 1km.

ACCOMMODATION

Price guide (double room per night):
Expensive: 130 euros upwards
Moderate: 60–130 euros
Inexpensive: less than 60 euros
(Note: 'Palace' hotels can cost at least 300–450 euros per night.)

Credit cards: Nearly all the establishments listed here take most major credit cards, though a few won't accept American Express – check when you reserve.

Antibes/Juan-les-Pins
Hôtel du Cap-Eden-Roc
Boulevard J F Kennedy, BP 29
Tel: 04 93 61 39 01. Fax: 04 93 67 76 04
www.edenroc-hotel.fr
Beautifully set on the water's edge in extensive wooded grounds with its own rock carved pool. Very luxurious, popular with Cannes film stars. Expensive.

Belles Rives
Boulevard E Baudoin
Tel: 04 93 61 02 79. Fax: 04 93 67 43 51
www.bellesrives.com
A 1930s hotel, in exquisite period style, once the home of Scott and Zelda Fitzgerald. Balconies and private beach. Closed 11 Nov–9 Mar. Moderate–expensive.

Beaulieu
La Réserve de Beaulieu
5 Boulevard du Général Leclerc
Tel: 04 93 01 00 01. Fax: 04 93 01 28 99
www.reservebeaulieu.com
Luxurious Renaissance-style pink villa dominating the seafront. Private beach and celebrated restaurant. Expensive.

Cagnes
Le Cagnard
45 Rue Sous Bari, Haut-de-Cagnes
Tel: 04 93 20 73 22. Fax: 04 93 22 06 39
www.le-cagnard.com
An exquisite little hotel in the heart of the old village near Grimaldi castle, with romantic beamed bedrooms and an excellent restaurant. Expensive.

practical information

Cannes
Carlton Inter-Continental
58 La Croisette, BP 155
Tel: 04 93 06 40 06. Fax: 04 93 06 40 25
cannes.interconti.com
Glamorous Croisette hotel, the most celebrated place to stay during the Cannes film festival. Expensive.

Hôtel Martinez
73 La Croisette
Tel: 04 92 98 73 00. Fax: 04 93 39 67 82
www.hotel-martinez.com
Fabulous Art Deco hotel with private beach and gigantic pool, and one of the best restaurants in Cannes. Expensive.

Cap Ferrat
Brise Marine
58 Avenue Jean Mermoz,
St Jean-Cap-Ferrat
Tel: 04 93 76 04 36. Fax: 04 93 76 11 49
www.hotel-brisemarine.com
Sweet hotel in superb location, with some rooms overlooking the sea and a pretty terraced garden. Closed 1 Nov–31 Jan. Moderate.

La Voile d'Or
7 Avenue J Mermoz, Port de St Jean
Tel: 04 93 01 13 13. Fax: 04 93 76 11 17
www.lavoiledor.fr
Italian-style villa with pools, in a garden overlooking the harbour. Attractive rooms and good restaurant. Expensive.

Eze
Château Eza
Rue de la Pise
Tel: 04 93 41 12 24. Fax: 04 93 41 16 64
www.slh.com/eza
This fabulous castle hotel perched on the rocks has antique furnishings, stunning ocean views and a celebrated restaurant. Expensive.

Fréjus
Résidence du Colombier
Route des Ancients Combattants d'Afrique du Nord
Tel: 04 94 51 45 92. Fax: 04 94 53 82 85
Separate villas with private terraces surrounded by pine woods. Swimming pool and sports facilities. Closed 1 Nov–31 Jan. Inexpensive.

Menton
Chambord
6 Avenue Boyer
Tel: 04 93 35 94 19. Fax: 04 93 41 30 55
www.hotel-chambord.com
Reasonable and well-situated option, just off the Promenade de Soleil. No restaurant. Moderate.

Hôtel de Londres
15 Avenue Carnot
Tel: 04 93 35 74 62. Fax: 04 93 41 77 78
www.hotel-de-londres.com
Small, convenient hotel in the centre of Menton. Inexpensive.

Monaco
Columbus Hotel
23 Avenue des Papalins, Fontvielle
Tel: 377-92 05 90 00. Fax: 377-92 05 91 67
www.columbushotels.com
A comfortable modern hotel overlooking the new harbour and situated out of the centre. Expensive.

Hôtel de Paris
Place du Casino, Monte Carlo
Tel: 377-92 16 30 00. Fax: 377-92 16 38 49
Monaco's most famous hotel, offering the ultimate in luxury including Alain Ducasse's celebrated restaurant and an indoor swimming pool. Expensive.

Hôtel Hermitage
Place Beaumarchais, Monte Carlo
Tel: 377-92 16 40 00. Fax: 377-92 16 40 17
Email: resort@sbm.mc
Total luxury in gorgeous Belle Epoque building with glass domed winter garden, baroque dining room and wonderful terrace. Swimming pool and fitness centre. Expensive.

Hôtel Mirabeau
1 Avenue Princess Grace, Monte Carlo
Tel: 377-92 16 65 65. Fax: 377-92 16 40 19
Email: resort@sbm.mc
Another magnificent hotel with its own garden, swimming pool, and two restaurants, including the Michelin starred La Coupole. Expensive.

Metropole Palace
4 Avenue de la Madone, Monte Carlo
Tel: 377-93 15 15 15. Fax: 377-93 25 24 44
www.metropole.mc
Discreetly luxurious Monaco hotel with Belle Epoque frescoes in the lobby and every comfort provided for. Expensive.

Mougins
Le Mas Candille
Boulevard Clément Rebuffel
Tel: 04 92 28 43 43. Fax: 04 92 28 43 40
www.lemascandille.com
Old *mas* outside Mougins, with pool and terrace with mountain views. Expensive.

Nice
Hôtel Negresco
37 Promenade des Anglais
Tel: 04 93 16 64 00. Fax: 04 93 88 35 68
www.hotel-negresco-nice.com
This is Nice's most glorious hotel, its great pink dome dominating the Promenade des Anglais. Every luxury and impeccable service. Expensive.

Hôtel Windsor
11 Rue Dalpozzo
Tel: 04 93 88 59 35. Fax: 04 93 88 94 57
www.hotelwindsornice.com
A very cool, well-situated hotel with many of the rooms decorated by a different artist. There's a gorgeous, exotic garden with pool outside and an indoor hamman. Good service. Moderate.

Hôtel de Flore
2 Rue Maccarani
Tel: 04 92 14 40 20. Fax: 04 92 14 40 21
www.hoteldeflore-nice.com
Hôtel de Flore is situated two blocks from the sea, with a quiet courtyard and elegant decor. Moderate.

Hôtel de la Mer
4 Place Masséna
Tel: 04 93 92 09 10. Fax: 04 93 85 00 64
This is a clean, attractive and well-located two-star hotel; some rooms have balconies. Inexpensive–moderate.

Left: cool waters
Above: the renowned Carlton Hotel, Cannes

practical information

Palais Maeterlinck
Four miles/6km from Nice, direction Ville-franche on Corniche Inferieur.
Tel: 04 92 00 72 00. Fax: 04 92 04 18 10
www.palais-maeterlinck.com
Glamorous hotel on the cliff-side, with glass lift, pool. Most rooms with own garden or terrace. Expensive.

Peillon
Auberge de la Madone
2 Place Auguste Arnulf
Tel: 04 93 79 91 17. Fax: 04 93 79 99 36
Simple hotel in hilltop village with rooms offering splendid views. Moderate.

Roquebrune
Vista Palace Hotel
Route de la Grande Corniche
Tel: 04 92 10 40 00. Fax: 04 93 35 18 94
www.vistapalace.com
Modern luxury hotel set above Monaco; there are spacious rooms and good views. Expensive.

St Paul-de-Vence
Colombe d'Or
Place Général de Gaulle
Tel: 04 93 32 80 02. Fax: 04 93 32 77 78
Lovely old hotel, once frequented by Picasso, whose works still adorn the walls. Private courtyard and swimming pool. Closed 2 Nov–20 Dec. Expensive.

Auberge du Colombier
Route de Nice, Roquefort-les-Pins
Tel: 04 92 60 33 00. Fax: 04 93 77 07 03
www.auberge-du-colombier.com
Auberge du Colombier is a small, friendly hotel set in a beautiful garden with swimming pool, tennis courts and views down to the sea. Closed Jan. Moderate.

St Tropez
Lou Cagnard
Avenue P Roussel
Tel: 04 94 97 04 24. Fax: 04 94 97 09 44
Situated near the port, this hotel has a pretty courtyard. Closed 4 Nov–27 Dec. Inexpensive.

Résidence de la Pinède
Plage de la Bouillabaisse
Tel: 04 94 55 91 00. Fax: 04 94 97 73 64
www.residencepinede.com
Situated on the famous Bouillabaisse beach, offering comfortable rooms and suites. Closed Nov–Mar. Expensive.

La Ponche
3 Rue des Remparts, Port des Pêcheurs
Tel: 04 94 97 02 53. Fax: 04 94 07 78 61
www.laponche.com
A lovely hotel, created from a row of cottages, that was once a favourite of Picasso. Closed 3 Nov–14 Feb. Expensive.

Le Yaca
1 Boulevard d'Aumale
Tel: 04 94 55 81 00. Fax: 04 94 97 58 50
www.hotel-le-yaca.fr
Occupying a delightful old Provençal residence in St Tropez, Le Yaca has a pool and pleasant garden. Closed Oct–Mar. Expensive.

La Boulangerie
Route de Collobrières Ouest
Tel: 04 94 43 23 16. Fax: 04 94 43 38 27
Charming hotel in the Maures hills outside St Tropez, with garden and pool. Closed 10 Oct–Easter. Moderate.

La Ferme d'Augustin
Plage Tahiti, Ramatuelle
Tel: 04 94 55 97 00. Fax: 04 94 97 40 30
www.fermeaugustin.com
Lovely old farm with a beautiful garden and rustic atmosphere. All rooms offer views of the ocean. Closed mid-Oct–mid-Mar. Moderate–expensive.

Théoule-sur-Mer
Miramar Beach Hotel
47 Avenue de Miramar
Tel: 04 93 75 05 05. Fax: 04 93 75 44 83
www.mbhriviera.com
Classic Mediterranean hotel overlooking the Esterel coast. Facilities include a thalassotherapy centre, terraces and pools. Expensive.

Vence
Villa Roseraie
Route de Coursegoules
Tel: 04 93 58 02 20. Fax: 04 93 58 99 31
Small friendly hotel in a 1930s villa with a pretty garden and pool. Moderate.

Villefranche-sur-Mer
Hôtel Welcome
1 Quai Amiral Courbet
Tel: 04 93 76 27 62. Fax: 04 93 76 27 66
www.welcomehotel.com
Traditional hotel attractively situated on the quayside. Jean Cocteau often stayed here. Moderate.

MUSEUMS

The seven-day **Carte Passe-Musées** allows unlimited access to Nice's municipal museums – which do not include the Asian Arts Museum and Chagall Museum – over seven days during a 15-day period. The Carte Musées Côte d'Azur (valid for one, three or seven consecutive days) entitles the holder to entry into 65 museums in the region. These *cartes* can be purchased at the ticket desks of participating museums. Entry to Nice's municipal museums is free for everyone on the first and third Sundays of every month.

ARTS & ENTERTAINMENT

There is a highy regarded opera house in Nice and the legendary jazz festivals of Nice and Juans-les-Pins take place in summer. Top venues include:

Nice
Acropolis: Esplanade Kennedy
Théâtre de Nice: Promenade des Arts
Théâtre de Verdure: Promenade des Anglais
Opéra de Nice: 4 & 6 Rue St-François-de-Paule (booking office open Tues–Sat 10am–5.30pm at 9 Rue de la Terrasse. Tel: 04 92 17 40 00).

Monte Carlo
Théâtre Princess Grace: 12 Avenue d'Ostend. Tel: 377-93 25 32 27.
Opéra de Monte Carlo: Place du Casino. Tel: 377-92 16 22 99
Ballets de Monte Carlo: Place du Casino. Tel: 377-92 16 24 20

SPORT

For information about hiking, horse riding, mountain biking, aqua-rafting and bunjy jumping contact local tourist offices or the Comité Régional du Tourisme, BP 1602 – 0611, Nice Cedex 1, tel: 04 93 37 78 78, email: crt06@crt-riviera.fr.

Golf Courses
Biot: Bastide du Roy. Tel: 04 93 65 08 48.
Cannes/Mandelieu: Route du Golf. Tel: 04 93 49 55 39.
Cannes/Mougins: 175 Route d'Antibes. Tel: 04 93 75 79 13.
Grasse: Opio-Valbonne, Château de la Begude, Route de Roquefort, tel: 04 93 12 00 08; Golf de la Grande Bastide, tel: 04 93 77 70 08.
Monaco: Golf de Monte Carlo, La Turbie. Tel: 04 93 41 09 11.
Nice: 698 Route de Grenoble. Tel: 04 93 29 82 00.
St Raphaël: Quartier de Valescure. Tel: 04 94 82 40 46.

Above: St Tropez harbour

practical information

Horse Riding
La Colle sur Loup: Route de Montgros.
Tel: 04 93 32 68 33.
Mandelieu: Club San Estello. Tel: 04 93
49 36 26.
Nice: Crazy Horse Club, Chemin du Mont
Leuze. Tel: 04 93 01 84 11.
Roquefort: Chemin de Tourres. Tel: 04
93 77 51 64.
St Paul: Centre Equestre Patrone, Chemin
des Gardettes. Tel: 04 93 32 91 08.
Villeneuve-Loubet: Route de Grasse.
Tel: 04 93 20 99 64.

Hiking Paths
**Le Sentier des Balcons de la Côte
d'Azur** leads from Menton to the Esterel
along more than 40 different paths through
300 km (185 miles) of footpaths. Further
information on the specific routes covered should be available through local
tourist offices.

Water Sports
**Aigle Nautique & Club Nautique
de Nice**
50 Boulevard Franck-Pilatte
Kayaking, tel: 04 93 56 77 99
Diving, tel: 04 93 89 23 33
Rowing and sailing, tel: 04 93 89 39 78
Water Sports Centre
Cap 3000 beach,
St Laurent-du-Var
Tel: 04 93 07 53 73
Yacht Club de St-Tropez
Tour St Elme
Tel: 04 94 97 83 30

TOURIST OFFICES

Nice
Office de Tourisme et des Congrès
'Acropolis', 1 Esplanade Kennedy, 06302
Nice Cedex 04 (written enquiries only).
Tel: 04 93 92 82 82. Fax: 04 93 92 80 85
Website: www.nicetourism.com
Email: info@nicetourism.com
and (for visits in person) 5 Promenade des
Anglais, 06000 Nice
Tel: 08 92 70 74 07 (rate charged per minute)

Monaco
**Direction du Tourisme et des Congrés
de la Principauté de Monaco**
2a Boulevard des Moulins, Monte Carlo,
MC 98030 Monaco Cedex
Tel: 377-92 16 61 16
Fax: 377-92 16 60 00
Email: dtc@monaco-congres.com
Website: www.monaco-tourisme.com

Cannes
Office de Tourisme
Palais des Festivals Congrès, La Croisette,
BP 272, 06403 Cannes Cedex.
Email: tourisme@semec.com
Website: www.cannes.fr
Tel: 04 93 39 24 53. Fax: 04 93 99 37 06

FURTHER READING
Tender is the Night, Scott, F. Fitzgerald.
A Table in Provence, Lislie Forbes.
*The Perched Villages of the Alpes-Mar-
itimes*, S & E Guinsberg.
*The Oxford Companion to French Liter-
ature*, Sir Paul Harvey and J E Heseltine.
When the Riviera was Ours, Patrick
Howarth. History of the development of
the Riviera as a tourist resort.
France: A History in Art. Bradley Smith.
A history through they eyes of artists.

Other Insight Guides
More than 20 other books from Apa
Publications cover destinations in France,
including Pocket Guides to Paris, Alsace,
Provence, Brittany, the Loire Valley and
Corsica, each with a pullout map.

Right: a free ride home

Also from Insight Guides...

Insight Guides is the classic series, providing the complete picture with expert and informative text and stunning photography. Each book is an ideal travel planner, a reliable on-the-spot companion – and a superb visual souvenir of a trip. 193 titles.

Insight Maps are designed to complement the guidebooks. They provide full mapping of major destinations, and their laminated finish gives them ease of use and durability. 100 titles.

Insight Compact Guides are handy reference books, modestly priced yet comprehensive. The text, pictures and maps are all cross-referenced, making them ideal books to consult while seeing the sights. 127 titles.

INSIGHT POCKET GUIDE TITLES

Aegean Islands	Canton	Israel	Nepal	Sikkim
Algarve	Cape Town	Istanbul	New Delhi	Singapore
Alsace	Chiang Mai	Jakarta	New Orleans	Southeast England
Amsterdam	Chicago	Jamaica	New York City	Southern Spain
Athens	Corfu	Kathmandu Bikes	New Zealand	Sri Lanka
Atlanta	Corsica	& Hikes	Oslo and Bergen	Stockholm
Bahamas	Costa Blanca	Kenya	Paris	Switzerland
Baja Peninsula	Costa Brava	Kraków	Penang	Sydney
Bali	Costa del Sol	Kuala Lumpur	Perth	Tenerife
Bali Bird Walks	Costa Rica	Lisbon	Phuket	Thailand
Bangkok	Crete	Loire Valley	Prague	Tibet
Barbados	Croatia	London	Provence	Toronto
Barcelona	Denmark	Los Angeles	Puerto Rico	Tunisia
Bavaria	Dubai	Macau	Quebec	Turkish Coast
Beijing	Fiji Islands	Madrid	Rhodes	Tuscany
Berlin	Florence	Malacca	Rome	Venice
Bermuda	Florida	Maldives	Sabah	Vienna
Bhutan	Florida Keys	Mallorca	St. Petersburg	Vietnam
Boston	French Riviera	Malta	San Diego	Yogjakarta
Brisbane & the	(Côte d'Azur)	Manila	San Francisco	Yucatán Peninsula
Gold Coast	Gran Canaria	Melbourne	Sarawak	
British Columbia	Hawaii	Mexico City	Sardinia	
Brittany	Hong Kong	Miami	Scotland	
Brussels	Hungary	Montreal	Seville, Cordoba &	
Budapest	Ibiza	Morocco	Granada	
California,	Ireland	Moscow	Seychelles	
Northern	Ireland's Southwest	Munich	Sicily	

ART & PHOTO CREDITS

8/9	**Douglas Corrance**
6C, 7B, 24T/B, 30, 44, 45, 48, 51,	**Oliver Lentz**
53B, 54, 55B, 58T/B, 61B, 68B, 70, 84	
12T	**Nègre**
5, 13B	**Rex Features**
31B	**Topham Picturepoint**
2/3, 6T/B, 7T, 11, 16, 20, 21,	**Bill Wassman**
22T, 23, 25, 26, 27T/B, 28, 29, 31T, 32,	
33, 34, 35T/B, 36, 37, 39, 40, 41, 42T/B,	
46T/B, 47, 49, 50, 52, 53T, 55T, 56,	
57, 59, 61T, 62, 63T/B, 64, 65, 66, 67,	
68T, 69, 71, 72, 73, 74, 75, 76, 77, 79,	
80 ,81, 82, 83, 85, 86, 88, 89, 90, 92	
Front Cover Photography	**David C. Tomlinson/Stone**
Back Cover Photography	**Bill Wassman**
Cartography	**Berndston & Berndston**

© APA Publications GmbH & Co. Verlag KG Singapore Branch, Singapore

INDEX